American
English in Mind

Herbert Puchta & Jeff Stranks

Workbook **2**

CAMBRIDGE
UNIVERSITY PRESS

CAMBRIDGE
UNIVERSITY PRESS

University Printing House, Cambridge CB2 8BS, United Kingdom

One Liberty Plaza, 20th Floor, New York, NY 10006, USA

477 Williamstown Road, Port Melbourne, VIC 3207, Australia

4843/24, 2nd Floor, Ansari Road, Daryaganj, Delhi – 110002, India

79 Anson Road, #06–04/06, Singapore 079906

Cambridge University Press is part of the University of Cambridge.

It furthers the University's mission by disseminating knowledge in the pursuit of education, learning and research at the highest international levels of excellence.

www.cambridge.org
Information on this title: www.cambridge.org/9780521733502

© Cambridge University Press 2011

First published 2011
20 19 18 17 16 15 14 13

Printed in Malaysia by Vivar Printing

A catalog record for this publication is available from the British Library.

ISBN 978-0-521-73344-1 Student's Book 2
ISBN 978-0-521-73345-8 Combo 2A
ISBN 978-0-521-73346-5 Combo 2B
ISBN 978-0-521-73350-2 Workbook 2
ISBN 978-0-521-73351-9 Teacher's Edition 2
ISBN 978-0-521-73352-6 Class Audio 2
ISBN 978-0-521-73328-1 Classware 2
ISBN 978-0-521-73353-3 Testmaker 2
ISBN 978-0-521-73365-6 DVD 2

Art direction, book design and layout: Pentacor plc
Photo research: Pronk and Associates

Contents

1 My interesting life

1 Remember and check

Write *T* (true) or *F* (false). Then check with the text on page 2 of the Student's Book.

1   Brian is writing his blog at school.   `F`
2   He's worried about his future.   ☐
3   He wants to be a doctor.   ☐
4   He doesn't like flying in airplanes.   ☐
5   He's good at math.   ☐
6   He can sing pretty well.   ☐

2 Grammar

✱ Simple present vs. present continuous

a Write the verbs in the correct form of the simple present or present continuous.

Mom: Where's Alex?

Molly: He's upstairs. He ¹ _____is taking_____ (take) a shower.

Mom: A shower? But it's 7:00 in the evening. Alex always ² _____ (take) a shower in the morning.

Molly: That's right. But tonight is different. He ³ _____ (get) ready to go out. So, he ⁴ _____ (wash) his hair, too.

Mom: What? He never ⁵ _____ (wash) his hair. Well, not on Thursdays, anyway.

Molly: Yeah, that's true.

Mom: Just a minute. I can hear a strange noise.

Molly: Yeah, that's Alex. He ⁶ _____ (sing) in the shower. It's because he's very happy. He asked Ellie to go to the movies with him, and she said yes. He ⁷ _____ (like) her a lot!

✱ have to / don't have to

b Write sentences. Use the correct form of *have to* or *don't have to* and the words in parentheses.

1   (we / fly to Chicago)
    We don't have to fly to Chicago.
    We can take the train.

2   (Becky / go to bed early)
    _____
    _____ .
    She's leaving on a trip at 6:00 a.m. tomorrow.

3   (Oscar / study French at school next year)
    _____
    _____ .
    He already speaks it very well.

4   (they / get good grades in biology)
    _____
    _____ .
    They want to go to medical school next year.

5   (I / finish the project today)
    _____
    _____ .
    The teacher gave us three more days.

3 Vocabulary

✱ Jobs

Complete the sentences with the words in the box.

architect ~~dentist~~ doctor flight attendant lawyer pilot

1 If you have a toothache, why don't you go to see a _____dentist_____ ?
2 The plane landed safely because the _____ knew exactly what to do.
3 When my dad wanted to sell his land, a _____ helped him.
4 This house was designed by a very famous _____ .
5 While we were flying to Quito, the _____ dropped some food on my dad's head!
6 I had a terrible cold, so the _____ gave me some medicine.

4 Grammar

✱ like, love, enjoy + -ing (hobbies and interests)

a Circle eight hobbies in the word search (↓→↑). Then use them to complete the sentences.

1 When you need some exercise, you'll enjoy _____swimming_____ in our new pool.
2 I really hate _____ computer games.
3 My dad loves _____ around the park in the morning.
4 I like _____ to music to help me relax in the evening.
5 Tom doesn't like _____ fashion magazines. They're boring.
6 Ernie and his sister love _____ to the movies.
7 I enjoyed _____ pictures of my classmates for the art fair.
8 Max and Rebecca love _____ the samba at parties.

E	P	L	A	Y	I	N	G	R	I
N	R	I	N	N	O	N	O	U	N
R	E	S	W	I	M	M	I	N	G
E	L	T	I	R	R	A	N	I	N
A	Y	E	M	B	U	T	G	N	I
D	A	N	C	I	N	G	L	G	T
I	I	I	I	G	N	R	O	S	N
N	E	N	O	T	I	N	G	I	I
G	N	G	S	A	N	T	N	N	A
P	L	A	I	N	G	O	I	N	P

✱ Simple past: regular and irregular verbs

b Complete the story with the simple past of the verbs in the box. One word is used twice.

be bring drop give have order pick up put ~~take~~

Last week Tom's dad _____took_____ the family to a new restaurant. They ¹_____ a terrible experience. They ²_____ something called the "Exotic Surprise." First the waiter ³_____ some chicken and fries to the table. Both the chicken and the fries ⁴_____ awful. After that, he ⁵_____ them some little cheese sandwiches, but he ⁶_____ one of the sandwiches on the floor. Then he ⁷_____ the sandwich from the floor and ⁸_____ it on Tom's mother's plate! Tom's dad ⁹_____ very angry. They'll never go to that restaurant again.

✱ much/many

c Complete the sentences with *much* or *many*.

1 I don't have ___*many*___ friends at school.

2 Our teacher didn't give us _____ homework today.

3 How _____ bedrooms are there in your house?

4 There aren't _____ good places to go in this town for fun.

5 She works really hard, but she doesn't earn _____ money.

6 How _____ food is there in the refrigerator?

✱ some/any

d Look at the picture and write sentences.

1 *There are some eggs.* _____

2 _____

3 _____

4 _____

5 _____

6 _____

7 _____

8 _____

✱ Comparative and superlative adjectives

e Underline the correct words.

1 Lucy's very *tall / tallest* for her age. She's *tall / taller* than her mother.

2 That's the *smallest / most small* cat I've ever seen.

3 Do you think Dakota Fanning is a *best / better* actor than Miley Cyrus?

4 This is the *most / more* interesting book I've ever read.

5 Ruby got the *higher / highest* grade on the history test.

6 Which city is *bigger / biggest*, London or New York?

7 I love this game. It's the *better / best* one I've ever played.

8 We have a test tomorrow. There's nothing *worse / worst* than that!

⑤ Vocabulary

✱ Two-word verbs

Complete the sentences with *up* or *out*.

1 If you don't know what a word means, look it ___*up*___ in a dictionary!

2 I can't do this exercise! I'm going to give _____ !

3 Hey, Jenny. This new game is awesome! Check it _____ !

4 This math homework is difficult, but I'm sure I can figure _____ the answer.

5 I didn't like running, so I decided to take _____ swimming instead.

6 Culture in mind

Underline the correct words. Then check with the text on page 6 of the Student's Book.

1 Yarn bombers knit things like scarves and sweaters for *their friends / trees or statues.*

2 Some people say that yarn bombing is a form of *urban art / recycling.*

3 Most people agree that yarn bombing *does a lot of damage / doesn't do any real damage.*

4 Forensic science is used to *make old things new / investigate crimes.*

5 Forensic science *can be an interesting hobby / is only for professionals.*

6 Making a pencil holder from a soda can is an example of *yarn bombing / upcycling.*

7 Upcycling is a hobby for people who *ride mountain bikes / have good imaginations.*

8 The main point of the article is that *the old hobbies are the best / there are many new and interesting hobbies.*

7 Pronunciation

✱ Word stress

a ▶ **CD3 T21** Listen to these words. How many syllables are there? Which syllable is stressed? Write the words in the correct column.

architect   decisions   decoration
expensive   graffiti   information
instrument   probably

● ● ●   ● ● ●   ● ● ● ●

architect   ....

....

....

b ▶ **CD3 T22** Listen to the sentences. Then listen again and practice.

1 The architect designed a large and expensive building for the art museum.

2 In my opinion, graffiti is not a form of decoration.

3 We need information about the instruments they need for the high school band.

4 They say they'll probably make the decisions tomorrow.

8 Study help

✱ Vocabulary: Using a word web

A word web is a tool that can help you remember words that are related to each other in some way. Write a key word in a circle in the middle. Then write other words around it. For example, here's a word web with verbs that we can use to talk about *a song.*

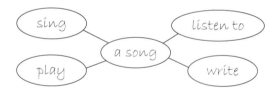

Practice making a word web of your own. Read Jack's description of his hobby. Complete the web with verbs he uses to talk about pictures.

I love to draw and paint pictures. Right now, art is just a hobby, but I hope that some day I will be a real artist. Sometimes I draw pictures with a pen, pencils or even with crayons. Other times I paint pictures with watercolors. I also spend a lot of time looking at pictures by famous artists. By studying their pictures, I learn things that help me with my own art.

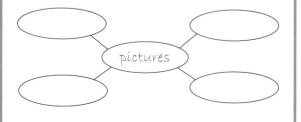

Skills in mind

9 Listening

a You are going to listen to a podcast called "The Truth About American Teens and Video Games." Before you listen, answer this questionnaire.

VIDEO GAME QUESTIONNAIRE

1 What percentage of American teens play video games?
  a 56% **b** 75% **c** 97%

2 Which group plays video games the most?
  a teen boys from 12 to 14 **b** older teens
  c teen girls from 12 to 14

3 Number these five game types in order of popularity for teens. (1 = most popular)
  .... Fighting games (Mortal Kombat)
  .... Music and rhythm games (Guitar Hero)
  .... Puzzle games (Tetris, Sudoku)
  .... Racing games (NASCAR)
  .... Sports games (NFL, FIFA)

4 How do most teens like to play games?
  a alone **b** with other people in the same room
  c with other people online

5 What percentage of parents think that video games are bad for their kids?
  a 13% **b** 19% **c** 62%

b ▶ **CD3 T23** Now listen to the podcast and check your answers.

10 Writing

Write an article for your school newspaper about video games and the students in your school. Include the information from the list below, and use the questionnaire to help you.

- how many students play games
- their ages and if they are boys or girls
- most popular kinds of games
- how they play, alone or with friends
- what parents think of video games

Unit check

1 Fill in the blanks

Complete the text with the words in the box.

| cans decorate garbage graffiti imagination knitting upcycle urban ~~yarn~~ |

Our school has a really cool art club. We meet every Wednesday after school in the art room and work
on our projects. There are many different kinds of projects. One group is working with ___*yarn*___ and
[1]_____ some very unusual scarves. Another group is studying [2]_____ around the city. They
think that it's a form of [3]_____ art. The principal is going to allow them to [4]_____ one of the
hallways in the school with graffiti art. I'm in what they call the "[5]_____" group. We collect old stuff
that people are putting in their garbage [6]_____ and recycle or [7]_____ it into a works of art.
Everyone in the group has a lot of [8]_____ . They have lots of great ideas. | 8 |

2 Choose the correct answers

Circle the correct answer: a, b or c.

1 Right now Harry _____ for fingerprints on his cell
   phone. He wants to find out who's using it.
   a looks for   b (is looking for)   c looking for

2 Don't call Jim at 9:00 p.m. on Fridays. He always
   _____ *Dancing Stars* at that time.
   a is watching   b watch   c watches

3 I don't always enjoy _____ in the morning,
   but I do it for my health.
   a to jog   b jog   c jogging

4 A taxi driver _____ a map of the city in his head
   and know where everything is.
   a has to have   b have to have
   c don't have to have

5 When we _____ home, we _____ tired so we
   _____ right to bed.
   a get/was/went   b got/were/went
   c got/were/go

6 Ask the teacher to give you _____ for your essay.
   a some idea   b any idea   c some ideas

7 He said this was a ham and cheese sandwich, but it
   doesn't have _____ cheese in it.
   a many   b any   c some

8 Ugh! That is _____ coffee I've ever tasted.
   a the worst   b the bad   c the worse

9 Do you think that English is _____
   language than Chinese?
   a an easier   b the easiest   c easier | 8 |

3 Vocabulary

Underline the correct words.

1 Hey, we have to *figure* / *check* / *give* out
   that new mall. It has hundreds of stores.

2 Do you think I'm too old to *give* / *look* /
   take up the violin?

3 To become a professional *architect* / *flight
   attendant* / *pilot*, you have to have a lot
   of experience in flying planes.

4 The *doctor* / *dentist* / *lawyer* is going to
   check your teeth.

5 *Apples* / *Eggs* / *Onions* are my
   favorite fruit.

6 Would you like some ice cream for
   appetizer / *main course* / *dessert* ?

7 He *dropped* / *fell* / *picked up* his ice
   cream on the sidewalk. | 6 |

How did you do?

Total: | 22 |

| :) | Very good 22 – 18 | :\| | OK 17 – 15 | :(| Review Unit 1 again 14 or less |

2 Looking into the future

1 Remember and check

Answer the questions. Then check with the text on page 8 of the Student's Book.

1 What do Tony and Ken want to do tomorrow?

   They want to play beach volleyball.

2 What does Jane think that her mother will say, yes or no?

   ....

3 What does Jane's mother say, yes or no?

   ....

4 What will Tony and Jane probably do on Saturday?

   ....

2 Grammar

✴ will/won't

a Look at the pictures and complete the sentences.

1 Grace thinks she _'ll go to the movies_ on Saturday.

go to the movies

Grace

2 Harry thinks it

....

rain tomorrow

Harry

3 Sophie thinks she

....

this evening.

go swimming

Sophie

4 Jack and Charlotte probably .... this year.

go to Italy

Jack

Charlotte

✴ too + adjective

b Write sentences. Use *too* and the adjectives in parentheses.

1 Paul can't get a driver's license because he's only 14. (young)

   Paul can't get a driver's license
   because he's too young.

2 Those kids can't use the playground because they're 16. (old)

   ....
   ....

3 You can't go into the theater now because the concert has already started. (late)

   ....
   ....

4 I can't wear those shoes because they're a size 6. (small)

   ....
   ....

✴ Adverbs

c Underline the correct words.

1 He's a _good_ / well guitar player.

2 She plays the piano very *good* / *well*.

3 He's smiling. I think he's *happy* / *happily*.

4 Sorry, I don't understand. You're talking too *quick* / *quickly*.

5 Please be *quiet* / *quietly*! You're behaving very *bad* / *badly*!

6 I'm really *bad* / *badly* at physics and chemistry.

✱ *be going to*

d Look at the pictures and complete the sentences.

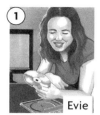
Evie

Mike

Alice

Cindy & Charlie

1 Evie's ___going to watch___ a DVD.

2 Mike _____ a book.

3 Alice _____ for a walk.

4 Cindy and Charlie _____ tennis.

✱ Future time expressions

e Complete the sentences with the time expressions in the box.

> the day after tomorrow   next month
> the week after next   ~~the next day~~
> in two years   in two hours

1 The museum was closed on Sunday, so we went back ____the next day____ . (on Monday)

2 It's 2012 now, and the next World Cup is
_____ .
(in 2014)

3 It's May. My birthday is _____ .
(in June)

4 It's Monday. The big basketball game is
_____ .
(on Wednesday)

5 It's 8 o'clock. I have to be home
_____ .
(at 10 o'clock)

6 It's December 2nd. The school vacation starts
_____ .
(on December 15th)

✱ First conditional

f Write sentences using *will* or *won't*.

1 We / go / scuba diving tomorrow / if / not rain
We'll go scuba diving tomorrow if it doesn't rain.

2 If / my parents / give me / money for my birthday / I / buy / a bike
_____

3 We / not win / the game / if / we / not play / well
_____

4 If / I / get / a good grade on the test / I / be / very happy
_____

5 He / not take / risks / if / he / feel / it's too dangerous
_____

✱ *should/shouldn't*

9 Angela wants to go scuba diving this weekend. Give her advice about how to ask her parents if she can go. Write sentences with *should* or *shouldn't* and the words in parentheses. Use your own opinions.

1 (do your chores and your homework before you ask them)
You should do your chores and your homework before you ask them.

2 (ask them when they're busy)
_____

3 (ask them when they feel relaxed)
_____

4 (be polite)
_____

5 (say that it's dangerous)
_____

6 (get angry if they say no)
_____

h Complete the conversation. Use the present perfect.

Sarah: Hi, Adrian! How's your vacation going?

Adrian: Fantastic! Chicago is the best city I __'ve ever visited__ (ever / visit). But it is windy! I ¹_____ (never / feel) such a strong wind, especially near the lake!

Sarah: ²_____ you _____ (ever / be) to Chicago before, Adrian?

Adrian: No. In fact, I ³_____ (never / be) to the U.S. before. Everything's awesome, but it's kind of expensive. Dad says he ⁴_____ (never / spend) so much in three days before! And tonight we're going to a Japanese restaurant.

Sarah: Japanese? ⁵_____ you _____ (ever / eat) Japanese food?

Adrian: Yes, lots of times. It's delicious.

Sarah: OK. Well, I ⁶_____ (never / try) it, but I believe you! I hope you have a good time.

Adrian: Thanks! I will! Bye, Sarah.

3 Vocabulary

✱ Adjectives for feelings and opinions

a Complete the sentences with a word in the box. There are two words in the box you will not use.

attractive	~~cool~~	dull	excited	exciting	interested	interesting	ugly

1 He's bought an MP4 player. It's so _____cool_____!

2 I don't like her new dress. I think it's _____ .

3 I loved the book. It had a lot of action, so it was very _____ .

4 The tennis game was so _____ that I fell asleep after 20 minutes!

5 Jim has black hair and blue eyes. Jenny thinks he's very _____ .

6 The program was OK, but I'm not very _____ in the history of architecture.

✱ Personality adjectives

b Use words from the wordsnake to complete each sentence.

relaxedlazymeanfriendlyhonestmiserabledisorganizedpolite

1 Angela's very upset. Julia did something very _____mean_____ to her.

2 Pam's feeling pretty _____ today. Her parents won't allow her to go on the class trip this weekend.

3 Frank held the door open for an older woman. Frank's very _____ .

4 I'm not a nervous person. I'm the opposite. I'm very _____ !

5 Luke knows everyone in the neighborhood. He's very _____ .

6 I can never find anything on my desk. I'm very _____ !

7 I'm not going to do anything at all today. I'm going to be very _____ .

8 That money isn't yours. Be _____ and give it back.

4 Pronunciation

✱ /ɪ/ and /aɪ/

a ▶ **CD3 T24** Listen and write the words in the correct columns. Then listen again and repeat.

> ~~city~~ kind think time tired tonight
> visit wind

/ɪ/	/aɪ/
city	

b ▶ **CD3 T25** Listen to the sentences. Then listen again and practice.

1 Can you explain why K-I-N-D is pronounced kind, but W-I-N-D is wind?

2 We're going to visit the city tonight and have a good time.

3 I think I'll be too tired to go out tonight.

4 It was very nice of you to think about us.

5 Everyday English

Complete the conversation with the expressions in the box.

> Don't panic   ~~all over~~   Just a minute
> Let's see   you'll see   You won't believe

A: We went ¹ _all over_ town trying to find the perfect shoes to go with my new dress.

B: Well, did you find any? What's in the box?

A: Shoes! ² _____ how much they cost!

B: How much they cost! Oh, no! I suppose that means they were really expensive!

A: No, no. ³ _____ . I meant they were cheap.

B: Well, OK, show me. Open the box.

A: ⁴ _____ . I'm going to put them on first. Then ⁵ _____ .

B: OK, OK.

A: Ta da! What do you think?

B: Hmm. ⁶ _____ . Don't they make your feet look too big?

A: Dad!

B: Ha! Ha! I'm just joking. I think they're cool.

6 Study help

✱ Thinking in English

In order to speak English fluently, you need to think in English. If you don't, your speech will be slow and it won't sound natural. Here are some things you can do to practice thinking in English.

● Look at objects around your home and school, and think of what they are called in English. Try to make a direct connection between the object and the English word.

= chair

● When you are out in a public place, practice describing the things and people you see in your mind. For example, think, "There's a man walking down the street. He's wearing a suit. I think he's going to work." Try to think in English first, not in your first language.

There's a man.

● When you have to say something in English, think first and ask yourself, "What words and expressions do I know in English that I can use in this situation?" Try not to think in your first language and translate your ideas into English. If you do, you will get frustrated very quickly.

Try these tips and you'll soon find that you are thinking in English.

7 Read

a Look at the pictures and the title of the text. Can you guess what the story is about? Check (✓) your guess.

.... Helping people who get lost when traveling

.... Finding lost children

.... Helping people who lose things

b Read the text. Was your guess correct?

Lost anything lately?

Where are my keys? Where's my cell phone? I can't find my math book. Does this sound like you or someone you know? If it does, here are two ideas that can help.

First, for about $79.99, you can buy something called a "Loc8tor Lite." (Loc8tor = loc(eight)tor = locator). Here's how it works. You put special little "tags" on the things you often lose, such as keys or a cell phone. Then the "Loc8tor" sends out a signal to find them. You can have four different objects with tags connected to each Loc8tor. It will find things as far away as 120 meters.

You can also try an Internet site called "TrackItBack." This website is for things that you lose outside your home. On this site, you can register items that you often lose, such as cell phones, passports and luggage. "TrackItBack" will give you an ID label for each item. You put the ID labels on each of your items. Then you hope that if someone finds the item, they will contact "TrackItBack," and you'll get your item back.

Or you could follow the advice your parents probably give you. Have a place for everything and put everything in its place.

trackitback®

c Read the text again and write L (Loc8tor) or T (TrackItBack) for each sentence.

___L___ 1 It is more expensive.

.... 2 It's free.

.... 3 It's good for things you lose inside your home or school.

.... 4 It's good for things you lose when you are outside.

.... 5 It can only work for four items.

WRITING TIP

Getting started

The hardest part of writing is often getting started. Students say, "I don't have any ideas." or "I have an idea, but I don't know how to say it." Here are some ideas:

● Talk to classmates and friends about the topic. Tell them what you want to say.

● Start writing with the first idea you have. You don't have to start at the beginning.

● Try to write for five minutes without stopping. Write down everything that comes to mind about the topic. Don't worry about spelling or grammar.

● Get up, go for a short walk and then continue writing.

These tips should help you write a "rough draft." But the work isn't done. Then go back and revise. Make sure your ideas are clear and check the spelling and grammar.

8 Write

"Lost anything lately?" gives ideas to solve an everyday problem using technology. Write an Internet article about a common problem and a solution. Use some of the suggestions above. Your article should contain:

☐ A description of the problem

☐ A description of your solution

☐ What materials or equipment you need

☐ How it works

Unit check

1 Fill in the blanks

Complete the paragraph with the words in the box.

> attractive   disorganized   hard-working   honest   kind   ~~lazy~~   mean   messy   awful

Maya's very smart, but she doesn't always do her work. She's a little _____lazy_____ . Frank is completely the opposite. He's very ¹_____ . But sometimes he says ²_____ things to the others and they get angry. Luckily Louisa is a very ³_____ person. She always has something nice to say. Her only problem is that she's ⁴_____ . Her backpack is always ⁵_____ , and she can never find anything. Today I drew some ⁶_____ pictures for our project. I didn't like them very much. So I said to the others, "Please, tell me what you think. Give me your ⁷_____ opinions." I was surprised. They all said the pictures were ⁸_____ .

| 8 |

2 Choose the correct answers

(Circle) the correct answer: a, b or c.

1 We were going to play volleyball this afternoon, but I guess we _____ play after all. It's raining.
   a will   b (won't)   c don't will

2 For Jack's birthday, _____ make chocolate cake.
   a I don't will   b will   c I'll

3 The teacher spoke very _____ .
   a loud   b louder   c loudly

4 Doug _____ some new sunglasses this afternoon. He broke his old ones.
   a 's going to buy   b going to buy   c 's going buy

5 Today is Tuesday, so Thursday is _____ .
   a the day after   b after tomorrow
   c the day after tomorrow

6 If Alex _____ rude to the other players, the coach _____ him to leave the game.
   a will be / tells   b is / will tell
   c will be/ will tell

7 If I _____ a new dress, I _____ to the dance.
   a don't get / won't go
   b won't get / don't go   c don't get / go

8 You sing very well. You _____ be nervous.
   a shouldn't   b not should   c should

9 _____ tried bacon ice cream?
   a Have ever you   b Ever you have
   c Have you ever

10 No, I _____ . It sounds terrible!
   a never has tried it   b 've tried it never
   c 've never tried it

| 9 |

3 Vocabulary

Underline the correct words.

1 The Lopez family just moved into a new house. They're very *excited* / *exciting* about it.

2 The girls were *frightened* / *frightening* when they saw the big spider on the path.

3 Going scuba diving was a *frightened* / *frightening* experience for me.

4 Jake worked in a summer camp for kids last summer. It was an *interested* / *interesting* job.

5 Wow! We won by scoring a goal in the last minute. What an *excited* / *exciting* game!

6 Nan's not *interesting* / *interested* in playing tennis in video games.

7 People were *surprised* / *surprising* when they saw the statue was wearing a hat.

8 That news is *surprised* / *surprising*. I never thought May and Jim would get married.

| 7 |

How did you do?

Total: | 24 |

 Very good 24 – 20

 OK 19 – 16

 Review Unit 2 again 15 or less

3 Great idea!

1 Remember and check

a Match the words in the columns. Then check with the text on page 16 of the Student's Book.

1	streetcar driver	ice skates	dishwasher
2	rubber	window	chewing gum
3	mice	produce toys	windshield wipers
4	after dinner	supply of potatoes	roller skates
5	summer	several broken dishes	mousetrap

b Complete the sentences with words from Exercise 1a. Check with the text on page 16 of the Student's Book.

1 A woman from Illinois invented the
_____dishwasher_____ .

2 Thomas Adams wanted to produce rubber.
He invented _____ .

3 One summer day, an unknown Dutchman had
the idea for _____ .

4 Mary Anderson invented _____ and
saved the lives of many drivers.

5 James Henry Atkinson noticed mice in his house.
He invented the _____ .

2 Grammar

✷ Past continuous

a Complete the sentences with the past continuous form of the verbs in parentheses.

1 I _was making_ (make) dinner for my family when you called.

2 My grandmother _____ (listen) to rock music on the radio when I arrived.

3 The cats _____ (sit) on top of the piano keyboard, so I couldn't play.

4 I _____ (draw) a picture of the teacher on the board when he came into the room.

5 We _____ (laugh) loudly, so we didn't hear the bell.

6 Mom and Dad _____ (dance) when we opened the door.

7 Nick _____ (try) to do his homework on the bus when we saw him.

b Look at pictures 1 and 2. Write sentences in the negative form of the past continuous. Use the verbs in the box.

> cook   sleep   reading   eat
> take a shower   ~~watch~~

Last night at 10:00 p.m. ...

1 my Uncle James was in the living room, but he _wasn't watching_ TV.

2 my parents were in the kitchen, but they _____ .

3 my sister, Jenny, was sitting by the bookcase, but she _____ .

4 my brother, Mike, was in the bathroom, but he _____ .

5 I was in my bedroom, but I _____ .

6 my grandparents were in the dining room, but they _____ .

c Write questions and short answers.
Use the pictures in Exercise 2b on page 14
and the words in parentheses.

1   my Uncle James / read a newspaper?
    Was my Uncle James reading a newspaper?
    Yes, he was.

2   Jenny / reading? (eat a sandwich)
    Was Jenny reading?
    No, she wasn't. She was ....
    ....

3   Mike / look out of the window?
    .... ?
    ....

4   my parents / make dinner? (talk)
    .... ?
    ....

5   I / watch TV? .... ?
    ....

6   my grandparents / eat dinner? (sleep)
    .... ?
    ....

d Write the questions. Use the past
continuous form of the verbs in
parentheses.

1   I called you Sunday night, but there was
    no answer. What *were you doing*? (you / do)

2   I saw you at the sports center yesterday.
    What .... ? (you /
    play)

3   I saw your mom and dad with a lot of
    suitcases. Where .... ?
    (they / go)

4   You put the phone down quickly when I
    came in! Who .... to? (you /
    talk)

5   I thought John didn't like Maria! Why
    .... with her? (he / dance)

6   I saw your sister outside the movie theater
    last night. Who ....
    for? (she / wait)

3 # Vocabulary

★ *get*

a Complete the sentences with the correct
form of *get* and the words in the box.

confused   home   angry   ~~presents~~
wet   dry

1   It was my brother's birthday last week. He
    got a lot of _presents_ .

2   Sometimes my parents ....
    .... when I don't clean my
    bedroom.

3   Tim didn't understand the math exercise. He
    .... very ....

4   I went for a walk on Sunday, but it started
    raining, and I .... very ....

5   Our plane was late, and we ....
    .... at 1:00 a.m.

6   You're very wet. Come inside the house and
    ....

b Vocabulary bank   Complete the sentences
with the correct form of *get* and the words
in the box.

together   a chance   ~~hungry~~   sick
a lot of pleasure   a phone call

1   When I .... _get hungry_ .... , I eat an apple.

2   When I .... with my friends,
    we often hang out at a shopping mall.

3   My sister .... from writing
    her diary.

4   The last time I ....
    .... was my 10th birthday.
    I ate too much cake!

5   I hope one day I ....
    .... to learn how to scuba
    dive.

6   Last night I ....
    .... from my English teacher.
    She told me not to forget my homework!

4 Grammar

✱ Past continuous vs. simple past; *when* and *while*

a Complete the sentences. Use the simple past or past continuous form of the verbs in parentheses.

1 While the teacher _was writing_ (write) on the board, Toby _fell_ (fall) asleep.

2 Kelly _____ (take) a shower when her cell phone _____ (ring).

3 While Lauren _____ (watch) TV, her dog _____ (eat) her dinner.

4 Somebody _____ (steal) Dave's clothes while he _____ (swim) in the ocean.

5 Jonathan's hat _____ (fall) off while he _____ (play) baseball.

6 While Erica _____ (sunbathe) in the yard, the cat _____ (jump) on her head.

b Join the sentences in two different ways. Use *when* and *while*.

1 I fell. I was playing basketball.

   I fell while I was playing basketball.

   I was playing basketball when I fell.

2 We were listening to music. The lights went out.

   _____

   _____

   _____

3 I lost my keys. I was running on the beach.

   _____

   _____

   _____

4 Somebody stole my backpack. I was talking to my friend.

   _____

   _____

   _____

5 Danny called. You were taking the dog for a walk.

   _____

   _____

   _____

6 I was getting ready for the beach. It started to rain.

   _____

   _____

   _____

c Complete the sentences with your own ideas, or use the pictures to help you.

1 When I came into the classroom,

   When I came into the classroom, some boys

   were fighting .

2 While I was using my computer this weekend,

   _____

   _____ .

3 While I was eating dinner last night,

   _____ .

4 While I was brushing my teeth last night,

   _____ .

5 While I was doing my homework last night,

   _____

   _____ .

6 When I left the house this morning,

   _____

   _____ .

5 Pronunciation

✱ *was* and *were*

▶ **CD3 T26** Listen and <u>underline</u> the main stress. Then listen again and repeat.

1 A: I was <u>waiting</u> for you.
   B: <u>No</u>, you <u>weren't</u>! You were <u>leaving</u> <u>without</u> me.

2 A: You <u>weren't</u> <u>crying</u>.
   B: Yes, I <u>was</u>!

3 A: She was sleeping.
   B: No, she wasn't! She was reading.

4 A: They were singing.
   B: No, they weren't. They were dancing.

5 A: We were doing our homework.
   B: No, you weren't. You were playing games.

6 A: I wasn't writing a letter.
   B: Yes, you were!

6 Culture in mind

Complete the summary about the history of listening to music. Use the words in the box. Then check with the text on page 20 of the Student's Book.

> popular   records   ~~bought~~   recordings
> paper rolls   radio   invented
> steel needle   wax cylinders   disks

In the late 19th and early 20th centuries, many families *bought* player pianos. These pianos played music by using perforated
1 .... , but you could also play them like a normal piano. When the
2 .... (the wireless) became
3 .... , player pianos began to disappear.

The first phonographs appeared more or less around the beginning of the 20th century. The music was on 4 ....
made of aluminum foil. When people listened to the music a few times, the foil broke. Later,
5 .... could hold longer
6 .... , and people could play them more often.

Gramophones were similar to phonographs, but they had the music on flat vinyl
7 .... The disks turned, and a
8 .... or a small diamond took the music off the record.

Sony 9 .... the "Walkman" in 1979. That made it possible to go for walks, travel or play sports and listen to music at the same time.

7 Study help

✱ Vocabulary: how to remember new words

a In your vocabulary notebook, record words in diagram form.

- Draw pictures next to the words. This will help you remember them.
- Add new words to your diagram when you come across them.
- Copy your diagram with your book closed. How many words can you remember?

b Write the words in the correct places in the diagram.

> vinyl records
> a wax cylinder
> a gramophone

1 ....

2 ....

3 ....

8 Read

Where is the true home of the hamburger?

The kind of beef we use in hamburgers, ground beef, was possibly invented by Mongolians over 800 years ago. But who first put the beef in between pieces of bread and called it a hamburger?

Three different cities in the United States all say that they were the first to invent America's favorite food. Some people say that Fletcher Davis, from Athens, Texas, invented hamburgers. "Old Dave," as people called him, was selling ground beef sandwiches at his diner as early as the 1880s. Some years later, they say that a group of Germans called his sandwich a "hamburger" because people from the German city of Hamburg ate this kind of beef.

Other people believe that the hamburger came from a different city called Hamburg – Hamburg, New York. At the 1885 fair in this American city, the Menches brothers were selling pork sandwiches. When there was no more pork, the brothers used ground beef and gave the sandwich a new name, the "hamburger."

The third possible inventor of the hamburger was Charlie Nagreen, also known as "Hamburger Charlie," from Seymour, Wisconsin. He said that in 1885 he invented the world's first hamburgers at a fair. Seymour now celebrates the invention of the hamburger every year. In 1989, it was the home of the world's largest ever burger that weighed over 2,500 kg!

READING TIP

How to answer "true, false or no information" questions.

- Look at the pictures and title of the text.
- Read the whole text. Then read the statements carefully.
- Underline the parts of the text with the information.

a Read the text and mark statements 1–3 *T* (true), *F* (false) or *N* (no information). Then read the notes below and check your answers.

1 Hamburgers use a kind of beef called "ground beef." ☐

2 Mongolians invented hamburgers over 800 years ago. ☐

3 The three stories about the invention of hamburgers are all true. ☐

- "Ground beef" is another way of saying "the kind of beef we use in hamburgers." So 1 is *true*.
- The Mongolians invented ground beef over 800 years ago, not hamburgers. So 2 is *false*.
- The cities say their stories are true, but we don't know if the stories are really true, because the text does not give enough information. So for 3, *no information* is the correct answer.

b Read the rest of the text again. For statements 1–5, write *T* (true), *F* (false) or *N* (no information).

1 Fletcher Davis gave the name "hamburger" to his ground beef sandwich. `F`

2 "Old Dave" visited Hamburg in Germany. ☐

3 There is a city called Hamburg in New York. ☐

4 The Menches brothers used beef in their sandwiches because no one liked pork. ☐

5 "Hamburger Charlie" and the Menches brothers say they invented hamburgers in the same year. ☐

9 Listen

▶ **CD3 T27** Listen and check (✓) the correct picture.

1 What did Thomas Adams invent?

a ✓ b ☐ c ☐

2 What did "Old Dave" say he also invented?

a ☐ b ☐ c ☐

3 What did the man in England invent in 1750?

a ☐ b ☐ c ☐

4 What did the Menches brothers say they also invented?

a  ☐ b ☐ c ☐

Unit check

1 Fill in the blanks

Complete the text with the words in the box.

get   was getting   got wet   got a terrible surprise   got to school   ~~got up~~   didn't get   got nervous   didn't hear   was shining

Yesterday wasn't my best day. First I ___got up___ late because I [1] _____ the alarm clock. Maybe I should [2] _____ two alarm clocks! When I finally [3] _____ at nine thirty, I [4] _____ . My class was taking a French test! I [5] _____ because I only had 20 minutes to finish the test. Unfortunately, I [6] _____ a single answer right! After school I felt better, because the sun [7] _____ ! But when I [8] _____ close to home, it suddenly started to rain, so of course I [9] _____ !

9

2 Choose the correct answers

Circle the correct answer: a, b or c.

1 Our dog ran away while I _____ to Sarah.

  a talk b talked c (was talking)

2 We were in the yard when it _____ to rain.

  a was started b started c was starting

3 Jane _____ angry yesterday because we were late.

  a getting b gets c got

4 When I _____ about the prize, I got excited.

  a heard b were hearing c was hearing

5 The girls _____ when they saw the funny movie.

  a laughed b was laughing c were laughing

6 I saw Alice a minute ago. She _____ on her cell phone.

  a was talking b talked c were talking

7 When Lucas and Austin _____ , we were all watching TV.

  a arrived b arriving c were arriving

8 The phone _____ , so I sent her an email.

  a wasn't working b weren't working

  c didn't worked

9 When I got to the party, my friends _____ a great time.

  a was having b had c were having

8

3 Vocabulary

Complete the sentences with the words in the box.

windshield wipers   invented   engine   remote control   idea   a chance   ~~dishwasher~~   surprise   got to

1 Our new ___dishwasher___ is not as noisy as the old one.

2 Where is the _____ ? I want to change the channel on the TV.

3 It's starting to rain. Drive carefully and turn on the _____ .

4 They have a diesel _____ to produce their own electricity.

5 Josephine Cochrane hated doing the dishes, so she _____ the dishwasher.

6 Our plane was delayed, so we _____ Istanbul very late.

7 While I was listening to my favorite piece of music, I suddenly got an _____ .

8 I'll call you as soon as I get _____ .

9 My uncle lives in Australia, so when he arrived at our house, we got a real _____ !

8

How did you do?

Total: 25

| 🙂 | Very good 25 – 20 | 😐 | OK 19 – 16 | 🙁 | Review Unit 3 again 15 or less |

4 He ran faster.

1 Remember and check

Complete the sentences with the words in the box. Then check with the information on page 22 of the Student's Book.

> shorter   ~~fastest~~   best
> slower   more than

1 In the 2008 Olympics, Usain Bolt from Jamaica was the __fastest__ man in the 200-meter sprint.

2 Brazilian sprinter Lucas Prado was only a little .... , but he won gold, too.

3 In the women's javelin throw, Jen Velazco's throw was .... than Christina Obergföll's, but they both won bronze.

4 Lucas Prado and Jeny Velazco were two of the .... athletes in the Paralympic Games.

5 At the Paralympics in Beijing, there were .... 4,000 athletes.

2 Grammar

✷ Comparative and superlative adjectives

a Circle the correct words.

1 She's *more younger / younger* than she looks.

2 This is *the worst / the most bad* day of my life!

3 Who is *the older / the oldest* man in the world?

4 My brother's *much neater / neatest* than me.

5 Is your house *more old / older* than mine?

6 I think Giacomo is *smarter than / the smartest* boy in the class.

b Complete the sentences. Use the comparative (+ *than*) or superlative form of the adjectives in the box.

> tall   happy   ~~beautiful~~   good
> expensive   successful

1 My city is __the most beautiful__ city in the world!

2 The day I married your mother was wonderful. It was .... day of my life!

3 Is the Sears Tower .... the Empire State Building?

4 That was a great vacation! It was much .... our last vacation.

5 It cost $2,500! It was .... camera in the store.

6 Bill Gates is one of .... businessmen in the world.

✷ Intensifiers with comparatives

c Write a sentence about each picture in your notebook. Use the comparative and *much, a lot* or *a little*.

The steak is a little more expensive than the chicken.

1

A   B

10 dollars   9 dollars

2

A   B

Today: 16°C   Yesterday: 21°C

3

A   B

Ferrari, 230 km/h   Fiat, 150 km/h

4

A   B

Mrs. James, 32   Mr. James, 51

3 Vocabulary

✱ Antonyms

a Complete the puzzle. Write the antonyms of the adjectives that the pictures show.

```
1 G O O D
      2     G
         3
4              L
      5
         6  H
      7
      8
      9  E
```

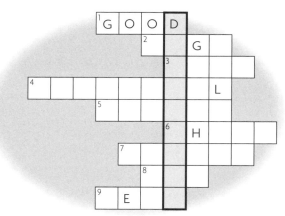

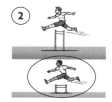

b What is the antonym of the mystery word in the middle? _____

4 Grammar

✱ (not) as ... as

a Match the sentences with the same meaning.

1 Cara isn't as tall as Riley.
2 Cara is as tall as Riley.
3 Cara isn't as short as Riley.
4 Cara isn't as old as Riley.
5 Cara is as old as Riley.
6 Cara isn't as young as Riley.

a Riley is 1.20 m, and Cara is 1.25 m.
b Riley is 15 years old, and Cara is 14 years old.
c Riley is 10 years old, and Cara is 11 years old.
d Riley is 1.65 m, and Cara is 1.58 m.
e Riley is 1.65 m, and Cara is 1.65 m.
f Riley is 15 years old, and Cara is 15 years old.

b Write sentences using (not) as ... as to describe the pictures.

Alyssa *is as happy as her sister.*
(happy)

John _____
_____ . (tall)

The TV _____
_____ . (expensive)

The cat _____
_____ . (thin)

The Australian team
_____
_____ . (good)

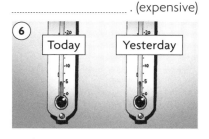

Today _____
_____ . (cold)

5 Grammar

* Adverbs / comparative adverbs

a Write the adverbs for these adjectives.

1 quick   *quickly*

2 slow   ....

3 easy   ....

4 happy   ....

5 fast   ....

6 bad   ....

7 good   ....

8 hard   ....

b Complete the second sentence so it means the same as the first.

1 His German isn't very good.

He doesn't speak *German well.*

2 He had to be fast to catch the bus. He had to run

....

3 He's a very slow driver. He ....

....

4 His writing isn't clear. He doesn't ....

....

5 My secretary's typing is quick. My secretary

....

6 The test was very easy for me. I did ....

....

c James, David, Lucas and Jackson all go to the same school. Read the sentences and complete the table.

1 The tallest boy is also the richest.

2 David runs faster than Lucas.

3 David is the shortest.

4 James is taller than Lucas but not as tall as Jackson.

5 Jackson speaks French better than James.

6 David is richer than Lucas.

7 Lucas speaks French the best.

8 James isn't as rich as Lucas.

9 The richest boy runs more slowly than David and Lucas, but not as slowly as James.

10 The boy who has $200 speaks French better than the tallest boy.

	James	David	Lucas	Jackson
Height: 1.5 m, 1.6 m, 1.7 m, 1.8 m				*1.8 m*
Money in the bank: $50, $100, $200, $500				
Grade on French test: A, B, C, F				
Position in school Olympics 100m: 1st, 2nd, 3rd, 4th			*2nd*	

6 Pronunciation

* *than* and *as*

a ▶ CD3 T28 Listen and write the phrases you hear.

1 *as good as gold*

2 ....

3 ....

4 ....

5 ....

6 ....

b ▶ CD3 T28 How do you say the phrases in Exercise 6a in your language? Listen again and repeat.

7 Everyday English

Complete the dialogues. Use the expressions in the box.

> guess what   that kind of thing   at the end of the day
> ~~an awful lot of~~   we're talking about   that's not the point

1 A: You want $200 for your bike? That's [1] *an awful lot of* money, Jake.

   B: I know it is. But [2] _____ a very good bike here, Andy.

2 A: That new girl, Sarah, is really good-looking. And [3] _____ ? Her father's rich, too!

   B: But [4] _____ , Paul. The important thing is that she's a nice person.

3 A: I'm going to be lazy next weekend and relax, read books, watch TV and [5] _____ .

   B: Good idea. [6] _____ , you can't work all the time, can you?

8 Vocabulary bank — Match the words with their definitions.

1 to tie
2 to substitute
3 a record
4 a championship
5 to score

a to take one player out of a game and put in another player
b the best performance in a sport that has ever been measured
c to finish with the same number of points/goals as the other player/team
d to win or obtain a point, goal, etc.
e a sports competition to decide who is the best

9 Study help

✱ How to get good study habits

a There are many ways you can practice and improve your English outside the classroom. Look at the pictures and mark how often you do the activities (O = often; S = sometimes; N = never).

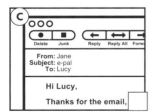

b Match the advice with the pictures. Write A–F in the boxes.

1 Eighty percent of the Internet is in English. You could try reading interesting texts in English, or find out about your favorite bands, movie stars and athletes. You could also try websites that help you improve your English.

2 Get an English-speaking e-pal and exchange emails with him/her.

3 Buy an English language magazine or newspaper regularly. It may not be easy at the beginning, but remember: practice makes perfect!

4 Buy or borrow a book that is the right level for you. Good stories that are not too difficult are a great help, and they're fun too!

5 DVDs are a fun way to practice your listening. With some DVDs, you can watch a scene in your own language first and then watch it in English.

6 Listen to a song by one of your favorite English-speaking bands. Write down everything you understand. Then go online and check the lyrics on the Internet.

10 Listen

▶ **CD3 T29**   Brody went to the World Cup with his dad. James talks to him about it. Listen and ⟨circle⟩ the correct answers.

1 What did Brody enjoy most about the game?

    a the soccer   **b** ⟨the penalties at the end⟩   **c** the stadium

2 How long after the end of the game did they leave the stadium?

    a an hour   **b** 30 minutes   **c** two hours

3 Where did they go afterward?

    a to their hotel   **b** to an Italian restaurant   **c** to a fast-food restaurant

11 Write

Rewrite the text to make it more interesting. Use the ideas in the Writing tip.

> It was 10 p.m., and I was late for the party. I got in my car. I drove to the party. A dog ran into the road. I saw the dog. I tried to stop. I lost control of the car. I hit a tree.

WRITING TIP

Making your writing more interesting

a Read these two descriptions. Which is more interesting and why?

> 1 Three years ago, I went to Germany to see the World Cup Final. It was a very good experience. We were very excited. We arrived at the stadium five hours early. There were a lot of people outside the stadium. A lot of the people were dancing and singing. We went into the stadium and went to our seats.
>
> 2 Three years ago, I went to Germany to see the World Cup Final. It was a fantastic experience! We were really excited, so we arrived at the huge, modern stadium five hours early. There were thousands of happy people outside, and a lot of them were dancing and singing excitedly. We went inside and couldn't wait to get to our seats.

1 Think about the language you want to use. Is there a more interesting or dramatic way of saying what you want to say? How does the writer in text 2 say: *It was a very good experience*; *a lot of people*; *we went to our seats*?

2 Add details to your writing. One way to do this is to use adjectives and adverbs. In text 2, how does the writer describe: *the stadium*; *the people*; *the dancing and singing*? Underline the adjectives and adverbs in text 2.

3 Too many short sentences can sound boring. Link some of them together with words like *and*, *so*, *because*, *while*, *but*, etc. ⟨Circle⟩ the linking words in text 2.

4 Try not to repeat the same words too often. How does the writer in text 2 say: *a lot of the people*; *We went into the stadium*?

b Rewrite the sentences to make them more interesting. Use the ideas in the tips.

1 She walked into the room and sat down in the chair. (tip 2)

    She walked into the dark room slowly and sat down in the comfortable chair.

2 My alarm clock didn't ring. I was late for work. (tip 3)

3 The meal was great. (tip 1)

4 My favorite restaurant is an Italian restaurant. The restaurant is the best restaurant in town. (tip 4)

Unit check

1 Fill in the blanks

Complete the text with the antonyms of the words in parentheses.

Mom got very angry at me this morning. "Your room is so _messy_ (neat). It must be ¹_____ (easy) for you to find your way to the door!," she said. I didn't say a word. I was ²_____ (noisy). My room is always ³_____ (messy). Well, there are some things on the floor. But the door's ⁴_____ (far) my bed, so it's really ⁵_____ (difficult) for me to find my way to the door. I think a neat room is ⁶_____ (interesting). When I look for my things, I always find something else. Yesterday, I was looking for my ⁷_____ (old) football helmet. I couldn't find it, but I found an old photo of my sister. She looked very ⁸_____ (old)!

⬜ 8

2 Choose the correct answers

Circle the correct answer: a, b or c.

1 Tennis is more interesting _____ football.
   a (than) b as c when

2 I read that women are _____ drivers than men.
   a as good b the best c better

3 He plays the guitar _____ .
   a well b bad c good

4 My Italian is pretty _____ , but I can't speak it fluently.
   a good b well c better

5 Tom is _____ I am. We are both 15.
   a old b older than c as old as

6 Read this book. It will help you to play golf much _____ .
   a good b better c well

7 This test is no problem. I can do it _____ .
   a easily b easy c easiest

8 People say Chinese is the _____ language to learn.
   a difficult b more difficult c most difficult

9 I live _____ away from school than all my friends.
   a farther b the farthest c far

⬜ 8

3 Vocabulary

Complete the sentences with a word or phrase from the box.

| as fast | most interesting | ~~more useful~~ | tied | zero | best | referee | messy | easy | dark |

1 For me, a new cell phone is _more useful_ than a new watch.

2 Meet Caitlin! She is my _____ friend.

3 The test was so _____ that it only took me ten minutes to finish!

4 In big cities, riding a bike can be _____ as driving a car.

5 My team lost, five to _____ . I can't believe it!

6 The _____ sent one of the hockey players to the penalty box.

7 Both teams played very well, and in the end they _____ the game.

8 Suddenly it was so _____ in the cave that we were all scared.

9 For me, geography is the _____ subject. I love it!

10 I should clean up my room. It's so _____ .

⬜ 9

How did you do?

Total: ⬜ 25

😊 Very good 25 – 20   😐 OK 19 – 16   ☹ Review Unit 4 again 15 or less

5 Our world

1 Remember and check

Match the two parts of the sentences. Then check with the text on page 30 of the Student's Book.

1 For a long time, Paris had a big problem
2 Now the Velib program might help
3 It allows people to take a bike and
4 You can get the bikes
5 One problem with the Velib program is that
6 Temperatures will continue to rise

a reduce pollution levels in the atmosphere.
b from one of the 1,450 bike stations.
c some people might steal the bikes.
d with pollution from exhaust fumes.
e unless we do something now about pollution.
f ride it for as long as they want.

2 Grammar

✱ *will/won't,* and *might (not) / may (not)* for prediction

a Match the sentences with the pictures.
Write 1–6 in the boxes.

1 Hurry up, Tristan. You'll be late!
2 Don't go up there. You might fall.
3 I don't feel well. I may not come to the party tonight.
4 I won't be long. I'm almost ready.
5 Listen, we're lost. I think we might be a little late.
6 Now just relax. This won't hurt.

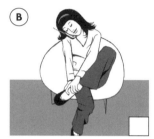

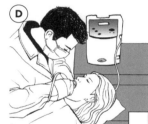

b Read the sentences. Then write *C* (certain) or *P* (possible) in the boxes.

1 People won't read books in the future. They'll only read on the Internet. **C**
2 Let's get this DVD. It may be good. ☐
3 You'll speak English really well after a year in the United States. ☐
4 I might see you at the party later. ☐
5 John won't be in school tomorrow. He's sick. ☐
6 Temperatures might not rise in the future. ☐
7 There may not be enough food at home. ☐

c Match the two parts of the sentences.

1 Is that the phone? John promised to call,
2 I might not have enough money
3 You won't have time to call Matt
4 I might not go to college,
5 There might be life on other planets,
6 Jeans will never
7 I may study Spanish next year

a because I forgot to go to the bank.
b before we leave. We're already late.
c but no one knows for sure.
d because I don't want to study anymore.
e go out of fashion.
f if I can find a good teacher.
g so it may be him.

d Complete the sentences. Use *'ll/won't* or *might / might not* and the verb in parentheses.

1   Maria __won't be__ (not be) at the party yet. It's too early. (certain)
2   I _____ (go) to the movies tonight. I'm not sure. (possible)
3   I _____ (not do) my homework tonight. I'm feeling very tired! (possible)
4   There _____ (be) some great music at the party. I'm the DJ! (certain)
5   It _____ (not take) as long as you think. Let's start now. (possible)
6   We _____ (have) time to have lunch before the game. (possible)
7   He _____ (not do) very well on his tests. He never does any work. (certain)
8   It _____ (be) a great concert. That band is awesome! (certain)

3 Vocabulary

✴ The environment

a Read the definitions. Then write the words next to the anagrams.

1	Wet, tropical places with lots of trees	arin frostes	__rain forests__
2	Dirty gas from cars and factories	fesum	_____
3	We find this in air or water	lotilupon	_____
4	The gases around our planet	rapseemhot	_____
5	A big building that produces energy	wrope oatsnit	_____
6	Using old glass, plastic and paper again	cringlecy	_____
7	Things you throw away	berggaa	_____
8	Pieces of paper, empty cans, etc., on the street	retilt	_____

b Match the two parts of the sentences.

1   If we want our planet to survive, we need to stop ⟶   a   recycle them!
2   Electricity is very expensive, so don't   b   pick it up!
3   Is that your empty candy wrapper on the ground? Please   c   polluting it.
4   Don't throw away your old bottles and newspapers! Please d   drop it everywhere!
5   Have you heard about the trees on our street? They're going to   e   cleaned it up.
6   People in my school don't care about litter. They just   f   waste it.
7   Our river was very dirty before they   g   cut them down!

c Complete the text with the words in the box.

recycle   ~~warming~~   forests   garbage   clean   fumes   pollution   cutting   picking   litter

It's ⟩Your⟨ Planet

Why don't you care about your world? Maybe you think there is nothing you can do to stop global
¹ __warming__ . You say that you can't stop people from ² _____ down trees in the
³ _____ . You can't control all the ⁴ _____ from traffic and factories that cause
⁵ _____ in the atmosphere. But you can do little things yourself. Can you say that you never drop
⁶ _____ on the streets? You could always try ⁷ _____ up the things that other people drop,
especially in our parks. They might learn from your actions.

Just think of all the money we'll save if we don't need to pay people to ⁸ _____ up the streets.
And there's no need to put your empty soda cans in the ⁹ _____ for someone to collect every week.
Why not ¹⁰ _____ your cans, bottles, plastic and paper? Then we'll all have a cleaner planet.

4 Grammar

✶ First conditional

a Complete the text with the verb in parentheses. Use the simple present or the future with *will* or *won't*.

How coral reefs die

Did you know that coral in the ocean will die if people _cut down_ (cut down) more rain forests? It happens like this. If people [1] _____ (cut down) more rain forests, the world's temperature [2] _____ (rise).

If the temperature of the ocean [3] _____ (go up), too, the small animals and plants that coral lives on [4] _____ (start) to die. So, the coral [5] _____ (not get) enough food, and then it will die and turn white. If the coral [6] _____ (die), over 90,000 different kinds of fish [7] _____ (be) in danger of dying, too. So, as you can see, one natural disaster often causes another one.

b Put the words in order to make sentences or questions.

1 you / pass your exams / if / not work hard
   You won't pass your exams if you don't work hard.

2 you / buy me a present / if / I / be good
   _____ ?

3 if / I / see / James / I / give / him your message
   _____ .

4 they / arrive / late / if / it / rain
   _____ ?

5 what / you / do / if / he / not call
   _____ ?

6 if / you / not have / any money / I / give / you some
   _____ .

✶ if/unless

c ⟲Circle the correct words.

1 I'll give you some of my chocolate ⟲if/ unless you give me some ice cream.

2 *Unless / If* you read the instructions, you won't know how to play the game.

3 Will you give Marco my message *unless / if* you see him?

4 *If / Unless* the phone rings while I'm in the shower, will you answer it?

5 Your dad won't be very happy *if / unless* he finds out what you did.

6 We'll be late *unless / if* we leave right now.

d Complete the sentences with your own ideas.

1 I'll go out this weekend if _____ .

2 If I get hungry on the way home from school, _____ .

3 I'll be happy tomorrow if _____ .

4 If the weather is bad this weekend, _____ .

5 I won't talk to my best friend if _____ .

6 If I can't watch TV tonight, _____ .

7 I'll make my own dinner tonight if _____ .

8 If I can't do my English homework, _____ .

5 Pronunciation

★ *won't* and *might*

▶ **CD3 T30** Listen and <u>underline</u> the sentences you hear. Then listen again and repeat.

1 They want to come. / <u>They won't come.</u>
2 They want to go to bed. / They won't go to bed.
3 I won't be here. / I want to be here.
4 So you won't play tennis? / So you want to play tennis?

5 I think you may be right. / I think you might be right.
6 You said you might teach her. / You said you're my teacher.

6 Culture in mind

Complete the summary about water with the phrases in the box.

~~for our survival~~ we cannot get to needs to be moist polar ice caps called evaporation have access to use one percent

Water is very important *for our survival* on the planet. Most water is salt water. Of all the fresh water, we can only ¹ _____ . The other 99 percent is in places ² _____ . Seventy percent of that water is frozen in the ³ _____ . Most of the remaining 30 percent is in the ground. The soil ⁴ _____ so trees and plants can grow. There are also huge underground lakes that we don't ⁵ _____ . When it rains, about two-thirds of the water goes back up into the atmosphere through a process ⁶ _____ .

7 Study help

★ Word formation

When you learn a new word, it is a good idea to learn the different parts of speech. English has many different ways to make verbs, nouns and adjectives.

a Look at these examples with the word *help*:

Noun: Can you give me **some help** with my homework?

Verb: Sometimes **I help** my parents cook dinner.

Adjective: Using a dictionary **is helpful** if you want to know the different forms of a word.

b A good dictionary will give you information about the different forms of a word and example sentences. Look at the example from the *Cambridge Learner's Dictionary*. What part of speech is *environment*? *noun*
What is the adjective? *environmental*

> ○━**environment** /ɪnˈvaɪərᵊnmənt/ *noun* **1 the environment** the air, land, and water where people, animals, and plants live *The new road may cause damage to the environment.* ➲ *See usage note at* **nature**. **2** [C] the situation that you live or work in, and how it influences how you feel *We are working in a very competitive environment.*
> **environmental** /ɪnˌvaɪərᵊnˈmentᵊl/ *adj* relating to the environment *environmental damage* ● *an environmental disaster* ● **environmentally** *adv environmentally damaging chemicals*

c Complete the table.

Noun	Verb	Adjective
¹ _____	² _____	polluted
energy	✗	³ _____
power	✗	⁴ _____
waste	⁵ _____	⁶ _____
⁷ _____	increase	✗
⁸ _____	warm (up)	⁹ _____
¹⁰ _____	¹¹ _____	recyclable

d Use your dictionary to check your answers.

Skills in mind

8 Listen

▶ **CD3 T31** Seth is talking about school. Listen and check (✓) the things Seth likes and put an (✗) for the things he doesn't like.

1 sports facilities [✓] 4 the length of the classes [ ]
2 school meals [ ] 5 the school uniform [ ]
3 the teachers [ ] 6 school rules [ ]

9 Read and write

a Read the text and answer the questions.

Make Greenville High School a better place!

Do you ever complain about school to your family and friends? Maybe about the classes, or the school facilities or the food? We all have bad things to say sometimes, but we can't just complain. A better idea is to say what you think is wrong and why, and to make suggestions so that things can improve.

Enter our contest! Write an article for the school website and tell us what you think is wrong with our school. Explain the problems, and say what you think we can do about it.

This is not homework! The best article will win **100 dollars**. So start writing now!

1 What things about a school do people sometimes complain about? Give three examples.

-- .

2 What do students who enter the contest have to do?

-- .

3 What will the winner of the contest receive?

-- .

b Read Jen's reply. Do you think Jen should win? Why / Why not?

-- .

Here's what I think. Some classes are really boring. All my friends say the same. My dad says why don't we have more classes with computers and stuff? I don't know if he's right or not.

And another thing. PE classes are boring. It's all basketball, basketball, basketball! I hate basketball. Why can't we do things I like – gymnastics, or dancing or something?

Oh, and I almost forgot. At lunchtime they tell everyone to go outside. That's crazy! What's wrong with people hanging out in the student lounge? Then we could play chess and stuff, or I could do my homework (or not!).

So, what about it?

Jen

WRITING TIP

Using transitions

Jen didn't win the prize! Her ideas are good, but her style is not appropriate. Writing an article is not the same as writing an email.

a Jen rewrote her article. Put the sentences in order. Look at her first article.

[ ] Second, not everyone in our school likes basketball.

[ ] Finally, why can't we use the student lounge at lunchtime?

[1] First of all, many people think that interactive lessons with computers could make school more interesting.

[6] To sum up, I believe that these things will make our school a better place.

[ ] We could have other activities in PE classes like gymnastics or dancing, for instance.

[ ] Some people want to play quiet games like chess, or just do their homework, but they don't have a place to go.

b What words does Jen use to:

● start her first idea?

● start her second idea?

● start her last main idea?

● give examples of activities?

● introduce her closing sentence?

----

c Write your entry for the contest.

Unit check

1 Fill in the blanks

Complete the text with the words in the box.

~~pollution~~   waste   reduce pollution   litter   pollute   may not   fumes   atmosphere   recycle   will

I live in a big city. There are a lot of cars and a lot of air [1] ___pollution___ . Near my city, there is a big factory, and the [2] _____ are a real problem. They [3] _____ the air and the water.

Today, we have big problems with the environment, but I think life in the future [4] _____ be really different. Cars [5] _____ use gasoline anymore. They might use solar power. More countries might [6] _____ levels by using clean energy, such as wind power. This will be good for the planet's [7] _____ . People won't drop [8] _____ in the streets or [9] _____ water. We will all [10] _____ bottles and other things.

9

2 Choose the correct answers

(Circle) the correct answer: a, b or c.

1   I think I _____ an umbrella with me.

   a take   b ('ll take)   c not take

2   I promise I _____ study all day tomorrow.

   a might   b 'll   c not

3   I don't think Krista _____ come to the meeting.

   a might not   b doesn't   c will

4   If she hears what you said, she _____ angry.

   a might   b are   c 'll be

5   If we _____ more rain forests, our planet will be in danger.

   a are cutting down   b 'll cut down   c cut down

6   Unless she helps me, I _____ her to the party.

   a might invite   b won't invite

   c don't invite

7   There'll be problems if we _____ cleaner sources of energy.

   a won't use   b don't use   c 'll use

8   What will Devin do if his friends _____ to him anymore?

   a don't talk   b talk   c will talk

9   If the weather is nice, I _____ and see you.

   a coming   b may come   c come

8

3 Vocabulary

(Circle) the correct options.

1   In some (developing countries) / polar ice caps there is very little clean water.

2   The pet food factory cuts down / pollutes a lot of our town's water.

3   People are cutting down / polluting more and more of the trees in the rain forests.

4   It took them a long time to clean up / cut down the oil from that beach.

5   They're building a new traffic jam / power station near our town.

6   We should do everything we can so we don't drop / waste water.

7   A lot of illnesses are the result of poor recycling / sanitation.

8   Recycling garbage / fumes can save a lot of resources.

9   Don't litter! Keep your environment / waste clean!

8

How did you do?

Total: **25**

🙂	Very good 25 – 20	😐	OK 19 – 16	🙁	Review Unit 5 again 15 or less

6 Holiday or vacation?

1 Remember and check

Circle the correct answers. Then check with the text on page 36 of the Student's Book.

1 Canada is ... the U.S., but only 30 million people live there.
   a as big as   b (much bigger than)   c not much bigger than

2 The biggest city in Canada is ...
   a Toronto.   b Vancouver.   c Montreal.

3 ... is a city in British Columbia.
   a Alberta   b Toronto   c Vancouver

4 The most popular sport in Canada is ...
   a baseball.   b ice hockey.   c basketball.

5 English and Chinese are the most common languages in ...
   a Montreal.   b Ontario.   c Vancouver.

6 It's about 1,200 kilometers from Vancouver to ...
   a New York.   b Los Angeles.   c San Francisco.

2 Grammar

✱ Tag questions

a Complete the sentences with the tag questions in the box.

> didn't they   can she   haven't they   doesn't he
> does he   can't she   aren't we

1 He doesn't know the answer, _does he_ ?
2 We're really late, _____ ?
3 She can wait, _____ ?
4 They knew all the answers, _____ ?
5 Your father works in that office, _____ ?
6 Your sister can't cook, _____ ?
7 They've finished their test, _____ ?

b If the tag question is correct, write (✓). If it is incorrect, write (✗) and correct it.

1 It's a nice day, isn't it? ✓ _____
2 He lives around here, isn't it? ✗ _doesn't he_
3 They're Spanish, aren't they? ☐ _____
4 Your brother studies math, don't he? ☐ _____
5 You went to Paris last year, went you? ☐ _____
6 They won't be late, will they? ☐ _____
7 She has a boyfriend, isn't she? ☐ _____
8 They shouldn't do that, shouldn't they? ☐ _____

C Complete the dialogue with the correct tag questions.

Steve: Jane, you play the guitar, _don't you_ ?

Jane: A little, but I'm not good!

S: But you played at the school concert, [1] _____ ?

J: Yes. Why?

S: You'll play at my party, [2] _____ ?

J: Well, OK. But Mike's going to be there, [3] _____ ? And he can play really well, [4] _____ ?

S: I think so. But that isn't important, [5] _____ ?

J: Yes, it is! He's much better than me, so you should ask him to play, [6] _____ ?

3 Pronunciation

✱ Intonation in tag questions

a ▶ CD3 T32 Listen and write the tag questions.

1 You're American, _aren't you_ ?   ☐ D

2 You're American, _aren't you_ ?   ☐ U

3 She goes to your school, _____ ?   ☐

4 They don't live around here, _____ ?   ☐

5 I can come, _____ ?   ☐

6 You'll help me, _____ ?   ☐

b ▶ CD3 T32 Listen again. Does the voice go up or down at the end of each tag? Write U or D. Then listen and repeat.

4 Vocabulary

✱ British vs. North American English

a Complete the table.

British English 🇬🇧		North American English 🇺🇸
1 _pavement_	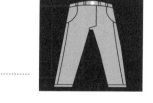	_sidewalk_
2		....
3		....
4		....
5		....
6		....

b Look at the pictures and complete the sentences.

1 John, can you take the _rubbish_ out, please?

2 Come on, Ann. Let's go up in the ....

3 I really like riding on the ....

4 Yea! I'm going on .... to Hawaii!

5 I need to buy some new ....

6 Hey! Don't ride your bike on the .... !

c **Vocabulary bank** Underline the North American English words. Write the words in British English.

1 I was surprised to see that my aunt didn't have any baggage. _luggage_

2 They're going to start building their new house in the fall. ....

3 Can you close the drapes, please? The sun's really bright. ....

4 There was a monkey sitting on the hood of our car. ....

5 Can you open the trunk of the car, please? I want to put the boxes in. ....

6 When we got to the bus stop, we saw a long line of people. ....

5 Grammar

★ Present perfect, *already* and *yet*

a Complete the table with the simple past and past participle forms of the irregular verbs.

Base form	Simple past	Past participle
be	*was/were*	1 ....
begin	2	3 ....
come	came	4 ....
drink	5	drunk
eat	6	eaten
go	went	7 ....
know	8	9 ....
see	saw	10 ....
write	11	12 ....

b Match the sentences with the pictures. Write numbers 1–6 in the boxes.

1 I've already eaten my dinner.

2 I haven't eaten my dinner yet.

3 They've already gone to bed.

4 They haven't gone to bed yet.

5 She's already seen the movie.

6 She hasn't seen the movie yet.

c Complete the sentences with *yet* or *already*.

1 I haven't finished my homework
   ....*yet*....... .

2 Have you heard their new CD
   .... ?

3 We've .... read that magazine.

4 She hasn't finished school ....

5 My parents haven't come back
   ....

6 I know that joke. You've ....
   told it to me!

7 They haven't had dinner ....

8 Have you brushed your teeth
   .... ?

d Write the sentences and questions. Use the present perfect and *already* or *yet*.

1 A: Alan, you / finish your dinner?
   Alan, have you finished your dinner yet?

   B: I / eat the hamburger, but I / not finish the vegetables.
   I have already eaten the hamburger, but I haven't finished the vegetables yet.

2 A: Maria / go to Brianna's house?
   ....
   ....

   B: Yes, but she / not come back.
   ....
   ....

3 A: I / buy the new Alicia Keys CD.
   ....
   ....

   B: Really? you / listen to it?
   ....
   ....

4 A: you / go to sleep?
   ....
   ....

   B: No! And you / ask me three times!
   ....
   ....

6 Grammar

✱ Present perfect with *just*

a Write *just* in the correct place in each sentence.

1 He's come home. *He's just come home.*

2 I've called Jenny. _____ .

3 We've arrived. _____ .

4 My parents have gone out. _____ .

5 The movie's finished. _____ .

b Look at the pictures. Write sentences using the present perfect with *just* and *yet*.

1 buy a magazine / read it

He's just bought a magazine,
but he hasn't read it yet.

2 buy some ice cream / finish it

_____
_____ .

3 write a letter / mail it

_____
_____ .

4 buy a new CD / listen to it

_____
_____ .

8 Study help

✱ How to remember verbs

Make flash cards that you can carry with you. Here is an example using past forms of irregular verbs.

• Get some index cards. On one side of each card, write an irregular English verb. On the other side, write the simple past and past participle forms.

> throw   threw, thrown

• Carry the cards in your pocket or backpack. When you have time, take a card, look at the verb and try to remember the two past forms. Turn the card over and check. You can use the cards to practice on the bus, during breaks at school and at other times.

7 Everyday English

Complete the dialogue. Use the expressions in the box.

> And besides
> behind her back
> How are things going
> No wonder
> ~~What do you say~~
> Why don't

Pete: ¹ *What do you say* we watch a mystery on TV? There's one on channel 2.

Amy: Sure, I like mysteries. ² _____ there's nothing else on that I want to see.

Pete: Oh, it's starting now.

...

Pete: Why is the woman looking out the window?

Amy: I don't know, but look at the man. He's putting something in her coffee ³ _____ . She can't see him.

Pete: Yeah, they always do that in movies. You know it's going to happen.

Amy: I know. It seems they never think of any new ideas.

Pete: I agree. ⁴ _____ it's so easy to guess who committed the crime.

Amy: This is boring. ⁵ _____ we turn it off and just talk?

Pete: Good idea. By the way, I wanted to ask you a question. ⁶ _____ with your new job?

Skills in mind

LISTENING TIP

Listening and choosing pictures

Sometimes you have to listen to a recording and look at pictures. While you listen, you have to either:

- check the pictures that show things that the people talk about

or:

- choose from sets of pictures that are similar to each other.

1   Look at the pictures carefully before you listen. What do the pictures show? What are the things called in English? If there are pairs of pictures, how are they different from each other?

2   Listen the first time. Do you hear any of the words in English that you thought of in question 1?

3   If you are sure about a picture, check (✔) it. If you aren't sure, listen again.

4   Remember: You don't have to understand **everything** to choose the correct picture(s). Listen for the **key words**.

9   Listen

a   ▶ **CD3 T33**   Josh has been on a trip to the U.K. Listen to him talking to Megan about his trip. Check (✔) the things in the pictures he talks about.

 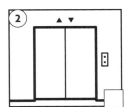

 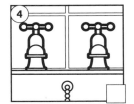 

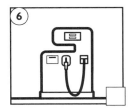 

b   ▶ **CD3 T33**   Match the words. Then listen again and check.

British English		North American English
1 bill		a truck
2 lift		b gas
3 tap		c check
4 petrol		d elevator
5 lorry		e faucet

10   Write

a   You are going on vacation to the U.S. You are going to stay with an American family in New York City and study English at a school there. Look at the list of things you need to do before you go.

A (✔) means you have already done it. An X (✗) means you haven't done it yet.

b   Write an email to your e-pal in New York. Tell him/her about your trip and about your preparations for it. Use the list and add more ideas if you want to.

Buy a plane ticket (✔)

Get a passport (✗)

Write to the family you are going to stay with (✔)

Write to the language school and reserve a place there (✔)

Get a letter from the school saying that you are going to be a student there (✗)

Buy some new clothes (✗)

Find out how to get from the airport to the American family's house (✗)

Buy a guidebook for New York City (✔)

Unit check

1 Fill in the blanks

Complete this email from an American teen to a friend in the U.K. Use the words in the box.

> apartment   have you heard   the kind of thing   take a look
> popular   subway   garbage   already   yet   ~~just~~

Dear Karen,

Guess what! I've _just_ bought a new CD by Selena Gomez. She's really ¹_____ here. ²_____ any of her music? I haven't listened to all the songs on the CD ³_____, but I think it's great. I love it!

My big news is that we're going to move soon. My mom and dad don't like our ⁴_____ anymore. They've ⁵_____ bought a house, and it's great! I'll have my own bedroom, and I can take the ⁶_____ to go to school. There's a photo of the house on my blog. ⁷_____ at it! Well, I have to go now. I have to take the ⁸_____ out. Ugh! It's ⁹_____ I really hate doing! Well, write to me soon and tell me how you are, OK?

Janice

| | 9 |

2 Choose the correct answers

(Circle) the correct answer: a, b or c.

1   Lisa _____ to Tom yet.

   a spoken   b spoke   c (hasn't spoken)

2   I _____ what I'll do on my vacation.

   a decide   b haven't decided   c decided

3   I haven't washed the car _____ .

   a just   b already   c yet

4   You've read that book, _____ you?

   a have   b hadn't   c haven't

5   The capital of Germany is Berlin, _____ ?

   a isn't it   b doesn't it   c hasn't it

6   I've just seen Kate, but I _____ to her yet.

   a haven't spoken   b didn't speak   c don't speak

7   Tony and Sarah have just moved to Lima, _____ ?

   a haven't they   b didn't they   c aren't they

8   You haven't bought a new car, _____ ?

   a have you   b isn't it   c haven't you

9   He doesn't live in Vancouver, _____ ?

   a doesn't he   b isn't he   c does he | | 8 |

3 Vocabulary

Find the words in North American English for the words in the box. (→ or ↓)

> ~~biscuits~~   rubbish   lorry
> pavement   flat   trousers
> sweets   lift   underground

V	O	T	R	U	C	K	A	C	V	E
M	C	J	G	R	W	Q	H	O	G	L
K	A	X	A	O	W	K	T	O	R	E
Y	N	W	R	U	S	K	Q	K	O	V
M	D	Q	B	B	G	L	B	I	T	A
Z	Y	H	A	D	K	A	Y	E	A	T
N	E	J	G	P	A	N	T	S	V	O
J	T	S	E	A	U	E	N	V	E	R
T	S	I	D	E	W	A	L	K	F	D
G	F	R	F	N	R	D	D	B	L	A
S	S	U	B	W	A	Y	S	Y	E	P
A	P	A	R	T	M	E	N	T	R	A

| | 8 |

How did you do?

Total: | | 25 |

| | Very good
25 – 20 |  OK
19 – 16 | Review Unit 6 again
15 or less |

7 Growing up

1 Remember and check

Match the two parts of the
sentences. Then check with the text
on page 44 of the Student's Book.

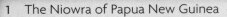

1 The Niowra of Papua New Guinea
2 When it is time for boys to become men, they are
3 The "Crocodile Nest" is a frightening place, full of
4 The boys take part in a painful
5 The boys play the drums together
6 When the ceremony is over, the boys

a taken to the "Crocodile Nest."
b ceremony that lasts for six weeks.
c to take their minds off the pain.
d crocodile teeth and skulls.
e are given adult responsibilities in the village.
f believe that crocodiles created the world.

2 Grammar

★ Present passive

a Complete the sentences with the
words in the box.

> is grown   are grown   's made
> are made   's written
> are written   is visited   are visited

1 My watch is cheap; it's _made_ of
   plastic.
2 A lot of coffee ....
   in Brazil.
3 The Hard Rock Café
   .... by thousands
   of tourists every day.
4 I can't read this book because
   it .... in Spanish.
5 Those computers
   .... in Japan.
6 Some cities in Europe
   .... by millions of
   people every year.
7 Millions of emails
   .... every day.
8 Oranges .... in
   many hot countries.

b Here are some signs in English. Match the beginnings and
endings of the signs.

1 English …
2 Foreign money …
3 Color film …
4 Fresh food …
5 Cameras …
6 English lessons …

a repaired here.
b developed here.
c given here.
d spoken here.
e changed here.
f served here.

c Signs like these are often written without the verb *to be*.
Write the complete sentences. Put the verb *to be* in the
correct form.

1 *English is spoken here.*
2 ....
3 ....
4 ....
5 ....
6 ....

d Rewrite the sentences using the present passive.

1 They collect 20,000 tons of garbage every year.

20,000 tons of garbage _are collected every year._

2 They sell a new computer every day.

A new computer _____ .

3 They design computer programs in that company.

Computer programs _____ .

4 People make mistakes in grammar exercises.

Mistakes _____ .

5 They build a lot of new houses every year.

_____ .

6 They often play baseball on Saturday.

_____ .

3 Vocabulary

✱ Describing a person's age

a Find and ⟨circle⟩ the words to describe people's ages. Then write them in order from youngest to oldest. Use the pictures to help you.

teenagerchildseniorcitizen⟨baby⟩toddleradult

1 _____baby_____   4 _____

2 _____   5 _____

3 _____   6 _____

b Complete the sentences. Use words from Exercise 3a.

1 In many countries, you become an _adult_ when you're 18 years old.

2 My older sister had a _____ last month. His name's Lucas.

3 My little brother's only eight. He's still a _____ .

4 It's great to be a _____ ! I can do a lot of things I couldn't do when I was a child.

5 My grandmother's 68, so she's a _____ citizen.

6 My cousin Jackson's only 18 months old, so he's a _____ .

c **Vocabulary bank** Complete the sentences with the words in the box.

> ~~come of age~~   getting on
> adulthood   look her age
> act your age   youth

1 In many cultures, when teenagers _come of age_ , they go through a special ceremony.

2 Come on, Sue, _____ _____ ! You're not a child any more.

3 My parents are still very active, but they are _____ in years now.

4 My dad always says that school rules were much stricter in his _____ than they are now.

5 _____ is a time when there are a lot of responsibilities waiting for you.

6 Your mom looks like your sister! She doesn't _____ at all.

4 Grammar

⭐ let / be allowed to

a Write the negatives of the underlined verbs.

1 We<u>'re allowed to</u> stay out late.
We're not allowed to stay out late.

2 I<u>'m allowed to</u> watch TV until 11:30.

....

3 You<u>'re allowed to</u> bike here.

....

4 The teacher <u>lets</u> us leave early.

....

5 Our parents <u>let</u> us play football in the yard.

....

6 My brother <u>lets</u> me use his computer.

....

b Look at the pictures and complete the sentences with the correct form of *be allowed to*.

1

Oh, no! We <u>'re not allowed to</u> take pictures here.

2

Sorry, sir. You .... park here.

3

OK, let's go, Jacob. We .... bike here.

4

Oh, no! We .... play soccer here.

5

I .... wear jeans at my school.

6

Sophia, remember that you .... eat or drink inside the library.

c Look at the pictures. Write sentences using (*not*) *let* (*someone*) *do* or (*not*) *be allowed to*.

1  **2**

3  **4**

5  **6**

1 Our father / play soccer in the yard
Our father doesn't let us play soccer in the yard.

2 We / wear jeans to school

....

....

3 We / run in the school hallways

....

....

4 My sister / our cat / sleep on her bed

....

....

5 My parents / me / put posters on my wall

....

....

....

6 Teenagers / go into that dance club

....

....

....

5 Pronunciation

✱ /oʊ/ and /aʊ/

a ▶ **CD3 T34** Write the words from the box in the correct columns. Then listen and check.

> ~~know~~ ~~now~~ show sound low loud around throw shout town house go down allowed

/oʊ/	/aʊ/	
know	*now*	

b ▶ **CD3 T35** Say these sentences. Then listen, check and repeat.

1 Let's go downtown.
2 We aren't allowed to go out.
3 Don't shout so loudly!
4 The kids are running around the house.
5 Can you pronounce this sound?

6 Culture in mind

Circle the correct option in each sentence. Then check with the quiz on page 48 of your Student's Book.

1 In Brazil, you *have / are allowed* to vote when you are 16.
2 In the state of Arizona, the parents *have / are allowed* to be present when a 14-year-old gets a tattoo.
3 In England, children can *have / must have* a bank account at the age of seven.
4 In Mississippi, people *can / aren't allowed to* get married until age 30 without their parents' permission.
5 In Japan, girls *are / aren't* allowed to get married before they are 16.
6 In the state of South Dakota, 12-year-olds *are / aren't* allowed to drive a car.

7 Study help

✱ Pronunciation: using a dictionary

a A dictionary can help you pronounce new words, if it provides phonetic symbols. Check the Phonetic symbols list on page 114 of the Student's Book. The letter(s) in bold in the word next to the symbol shows you how to say the sound of each symbol.

b Here are four words from Unit 7. Check their pronunciation in a dictionary. Look at the symbols for the underlined vowels.

all<u>ow</u> tr<u>i</u>be
cerem<u>o</u>ny bamb<u>oo</u>

c Now look up these words in a dictionary. Write their pronunciation using phonetic symbols.

mouse ....
though ....
straight ....
comb ....

8 Read

a Read this email from Mike to his friend Amy. Why is he writing to Amy?

○ ○ ○

Hi, Amy!

How are things? Hope you're OK. Sorry I haven't replied to your last email, but I've just finished my school science project.

Listen, it's my 16th birthday on June 17, and I'm having a party at my place. Can you come? Hope you can. The party will be great, and all my friends are going to be there. Let me know, OK?

See you!

Mike

b Read Amy's reply. Can she go to Mike's party?

○ ○ ○

Hi, Mike!

How are you? Hope you're OK and your project went well.

Thanks a lot for your email. It was good to hear from you. Thanks, too, for the invitation to your birthday party on the 17th, but we're going on vacation on the 10th and we aren't coming back until the 20th. I'm sorry, but there's no way I can go. But I hope you have a really good time and enjoy the party.

I'm really excited about our vacation because we're going to the Bahamas! Can't wait – it's my first time! A lot of sun and swimming, I hope. It'll be great! You won't get a postcard from me, of course. You know I'm too lazy! Well, I have loads of other emails to write, so I'll end here.

Take care and write again soon.

Love,

Amy

c Read the email again and write T (true) or F (false).

1 Amy and her family are going on vacation on June 17. | F |

2 Amy's family will be on vacation for two weeks. | |

3 Amy has never been to the Bahamas before. | |

4 She wants to do a lot of swimming on vacation. | |

5 Mike will get a postcard from Amy. | |

6 Amy has to write a lot of other emails. | |

WRITING TIP

Informal letters and emails

When you write emails or letters to friends, use an informal style. Study these examples:

- Begin the email/letter with *Hi* (name), or *Hey* (name). (You can also use *Dear* (name) for informal or more formal emails/letters.)

- At the end, write *Love, See you, Write soon* or *Take care* before you write your name.

- In the email/letter, use contractions or short forms. For example: *I'm* (not *I am*), *we're* (not *we are*), *he doesn't* (not *he does not*), etc.

- Show interest in the person you're writing to. Use expressions like: *How are things with you?, Is everything OK?, I hope you're OK, Thanks for your (last) email/letter*, etc.

- In very informal writing, sometimes *I* or *you* are left out, when it is clear who the subject is. For example, *Hope you're OK*, instead of *I hope you're well*.

Underline examples of informal style in the emails in Exercises 8a and 8b.

9 Write

Imagine you get an email from your American e-pal, inviting you to go and stay with him/her next summer. You can't go because you have planned to spend your summer somewhere else. Write an email to reply to your e-pal. Use Amy's email to help you.

Unit check

1 Fill in the spaces

Complete the text with the words in the box.

| child   baby   get married   let   given   ~~age~~   adult   toddler   senior citizen   allowed to |

What's the best _age_ in life? When you are a ¹ _____ , life is simple. You're happy if you are
² _____ enough food and milk and your parents look after you. Then, as a ³ _____ , you learn
to walk and begin to discover the world around you. When I was a ⁴ _____ , my life was great. I loved
it when I started school and learned to read and write. But I wasn't happy when my parents didn't
⁵ _____ me stay up late or watch TV. Perhaps being an ⁶ _____ is the best time in life. You're
⁷ _____ drive a car and vote, and you can ⁸ _____ , if you find the right person, of course!
Or is it best to be a ⁹ _____ , like my grandfather? He's 72, and he's always happy!

| 9 |

2 Choose the correct answers

Circle the correct answer: a, b or c.

1 How many cars _____ every day in the U.S.?

  a are produced b produce c produced

2 Too much energy _____ all over the world.

  a is wasted b was wasted c wasting

3 You _____ to sit here.

  a aren't allowed b isn't allowed c don't allow

4 His parents _____ go out on weekdays.

  a let him to b let him c are let him

5 _____ your brother let you borrow his sneakers?

  a Is b Does c Do

6 Some Australian animals _____ in any other country.

  a are not found b is not found c don't find

7 These days, cars _____ with the help of computers.

  a is designed b am designed c are designed

8 A lot of ice cream _____ every summer.

  a is eaten b were eaten c are eaten

9 Susan's parents _____ go to dance clubs.

  a doesn't let her b don't let her c allowed to

| 8 |

3 Vocabulary

Complete the sentences with the words in the box.

| underage   at least   grounded   youth   childhood   come of age   ~~baby~~   until   act your age |

1 My little brother is still a _baby_ . He can't walk yet.

2 My friends and I are all counting the days until we _____ .

3 She's not a very happy person because she had a difficult _____ .

4 I think in most countries you have to be _____ 18 to drive a car.

5 Stop playing silly games! You're 17, so _____ .

6 Dad says he played football in his _____ .

7 I can't watch that movie because I'm only 12. I'm _____ .

8 Lisa is really tired of being _____ when she stays out late.

9 In some places, you're not allowed to drive a car _____ you are 16.

| 8 |

How did you do?

Total: | | 25

| :) Very good 25 – 20 | :| OK 19 – 16 | :(Review Unit 7 again 15 or less |

8 Have fun!

1 Remember and check

Fill in the blanks with the correct words. Then check with the text on page 50 of the Student's Book.

1 Laughter is good for the _____health_____ of our minds and bodies.

2 Dr. Stuart Brown has discovered that play leads to the growth of more nerve connections in the _____ .

3 As children play, they develop their imaginations and become more _____ .

4 Amy Whitcomb is a teacher who uses _____ to teach math.

5 Some companies like Google believe that a _____ workplace helps their employees get better ideas.

6 When students are having problems with their _____ , they should take a short play break.

2 Grammar

✱ Present perfect

a Check (✓) the correct sentence in each pair. Put an X (✗) next to the incorrect sentence.

1 a Jon lives here since 1999. **✗**
  b Jon has lived here since 1999. **✓**

2 a I've had my bike for two years. ☐
  b I have my bike for two years. ☐

3 a A: How long are you here? ☐
     B: Since eight o'clock.
  b A: How long have you been here? ☐
     B: Since eight o'clock.

4 a I haven't been to school since last week. ☐
  b I haven't been to school for last week. ☐

5 a My mom has worked here for three months. ☐
  b My mom has worked here since three months. ☐

6 a I've seen that movie three times. ☐
  b I see that movie three times. ☐

b Clown Doctors are clowns who help children in hospitals by playing with them and making them laugh. Complete the text about a Clown Doctor. Use the present perfect of the verbs in parentheses.

Dr. Helen Marsden talks about Fran Mason, a Clown Doctor.

The Clown Doctor, Fran Mason, _has visited_ (visit) us every month since 2002. Little James Wallace is only five years old, but he [1] _____ (be) in the hospital for four months. He has a lot of fun when the Clown Doctor's here. James [2] _____ (have) three operations since last month, but he's getting much better. James's parents [3] _____ (tell) us the Clown Doctor's visits [4] _____ (help) him to get better. Since Fran's last visit, James [5] _____ (ask) many times when she's coming back. We [6] _____ (arrange) for Fran to come back next week, so James is very happy!

c Complete the questions. Use *How long* and the present perfect of the verbs in parentheses.

1 A: Maria and Marco live in Rome.
  B: _How long have they lived_ (live) there?

2 A: I have a new bike!
  B: Really? _____ (have) it?

3 A: My sister's in Paris.
  B: _____ (be) there?

4 A: My older brother works in that factory.
  B: _____ (work) there?

5 A: My dad studies Chinese at night school.
  B: _____ (study) Chinese?

d Complete the text. Use the simple present or the present perfect of the verbs in parentheses.

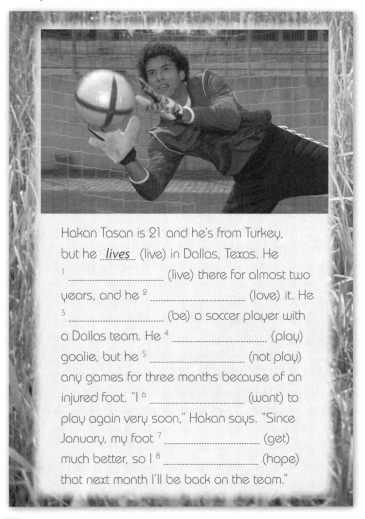

Hakan Tasan is 21 and he's from Turkey, but he *lives* (live) in Dallas, Texas. He
¹ _____ (live) there for almost two years, and he ² _____ (love) it. He ³ _____ (be) a soccer player with a Dallas team. He ⁴ _____ (play) goalie, but he ⁵ _____ (not play) any games for three months because of an injured foot. "I ⁶ _____ (want) to play again very soon," Hakan says. "Since January, my foot ⁷ _____ (get) much better, so I ⁸ _____ (hope) that next month I'll be back on the team."

3 Grammar

★ *for* vs. *since*

a Complete the sentences with *for* and *since*.

1 We've lived in this house _____*for*_____ a long time.

_____*since*_____ 1998.

2 My uncle's been here _____ Saturday.

_____ two days.

3 I haven't eaten anything _____ yesterday.

_____ 24 hours.

4 Our team hasn't won _____ six months!

_____ last July!

5 Andy hasn't called me _____ last weekend.

_____ a week.

6 I've studied at this school _____ a very long time!

_____ I was 11.

b Look at the pictures and write sentences. Use the present perfect and *for* or *since*.

1 Tom / be in the library

Tom's been in the library since nine o'clock.

Tom's been in the library for two hours.

2006   now

2 They / live in this house

_____ .

_____ .

Sunday   Tuesday

3 I / be sick

_____ .

_____ .

2008   now

4 My aunt / have her car

_____ .

_____ .

2007   now

5 We / have this computer

_____ .

_____ .

c Complete the sentences. Use the present perfect form of the verbs in parentheses and *for* or *since*.

1 Paula's hungry. She
   __hasn't eaten__ (not
   eat) __since__ breakfast
   this morning.

2 Tom's hair is too long.
   He _____
   (not cut) it _____
   three years.

3 It's terrible!
   My girlfriend
   _____
   (not call) me _____
   Saturday!

4 I'm bored!
   I _____ (not be)
   out _____
   yesterday.

5 Mike and John
   aren't happy. They
   _____
   (not play) soccer
   _____ two weeks.

6 I hope the
   movie's good. I
   _____
   (not see) a good movie
   _____ a long time.

d Write six true sentences about you / your family / your friends. Use the present perfect and *for* or *since*.

I've lived in this town since I was three years old.   *Carlo and I have been friends for three years.*

1 I / live / this town _____ .

2 I / have / (my computer / my bicycle / my dog / my cat) _____ .

3 I / be / friends with _____ .

4 _____ .

5 _____ .

6 _____ .

4 **Pronunciation**

✱ *have, has* and *for*

a ▶ **CD3 T36** Read the sentences and underline the words you think are stressed. Then listen, check and repeat. Pay special attention to the pronunciation of *has* and *have*.

1 Where have you been?
2 How long has he been there?
3 My parents have bought a new car.
4 James has gone home.

b ▶ **CD3 T37** Now read these sentences. Underline the words you think are stressed. Then listen, check and repeat. Pay special attention to the pronunciation of *for*.

1 He's been here for many years.
2 We've lived here for a long time.
3 I've had this bike for three months.
4 We haven't eaten for two hours.

5 Vocabulary

✱ Verb and noun pairs

a Complete the sentences. Use the correct form of *have* or *make*.

1 Last night's party was great! We really _had_ fun.

2 It's my birthday next Saturday, so don't _____ any plans.

3 I didn't do very well. I _____ four mistakes!

4 I fell off my bike and my friends _____ fun of me.

5 The class trip was great. We _____ a good time.

6 The Clown Doctor was _____ funny faces!

b **Vocabulary bank** Complete the text. Use the correct form of *have*, *make* or *take*.

Dear Annie,
I ¹_____ a problem. Next Friday, I have to ²_____ my driving test. I'm really nervous because last week I ³_____ an accident during my driving lesson. Until then, I ⁴_____ a lot of progress, but now I think I should ⁵_____ a break and cancel the test. What should I do? I have to ⁶_____ a decision today!
Thanks, Emma

6 Everyday English

Complete the dialogue. Use the expressions in the box.

in other words   What's the point of
come on   as long as
~~Tell me about it~~   Know what

Sharon: Hi, Ben. It's me, Sharon. Have you finished your homework?

Ben: Yes. It was really hard, though!

Sharon: _Tell me about it_ ! I worked from six o'clock until now! So, what are you doing?

Ben: Me? I'm playing my new computer game.

Sharon: Oh, Ben! ¹_____ playing computer games? They're a waste of time.

Ben: No, they aren't. You can learn a lot from a computer game, ²_____ you choose the right one.

Sharon: Oh, ³_____ ! You aren't playing the game because it's educational!

Ben: No, you're right. I'm playing it because it's fun. That's the most important thing right now.

Sharon: Ah! So, ⁴_____ , it's a game first and a learning thing second. See? I'm right. It's a waste of time!

Ben: Oh, Sharon. ⁵_____ ? I need to relax. So I'm going back to my game. Thanks for calling. Bye!

7 Study help

✱ How to learn English tenses

a You may find some English tenses like the present perfect difficult. Read these ideas to help you.

- Underline examples of the present perfect in the Student's Book and the Workbook. Do the same with any songs in English that you know.

- When you read, find examples of the present perfect. Think about **why** it is used.

- When you listen to your teacher (or other English speakers), listen for examples of the present perfect and think about why he/she has used it.

- Learn from your mistakes! It's OK to make mistakes and it's a normal part of learning.

b Read the paragraph below. Underline examples of the present perfect.

LA student wins trip to Buenos Aires

Mike Bennet, a student from Los Angeles, California, has won first prize in a competition for student computer programmers. Michael is 19 and studied at Berkeley High School in Berkeley, California, before going to the University of California in Los Angeles (UCLA). He has been interested in computing since he was 12, and he has already written several pieces of software. Michael has only studied programming at UCLA for one year. He entered the competition when a professor suggested that he could do well.

Skills in mind

How to answer multiple choice questions

- Read the whole text first, before you look at the questions and options. Use the title and picture(s) to help you understand the whole text. Look at the title and picture of the text on this page. What do you think the text is about?

- Read each question and the options carefully. Underline the most important (key) words in each question. Look at **question 1**. The key words are *Hunter Adams*, *went*, *Virginia*, *because*. Find the part of the text that has the answer. Words like *Virginia* are easy to find because they start with a capital letter.

- Read that part of the text carefully again.

- Usually there is at least one option that is clearly wrong because it states something that is completely different from the information in the text. In **question 1**, *a* is wrong because at the start of the second paragraph it says that Adams went to Virginia *after* he left the hospital.

- Remember: you don't have to understand **everything** in the text. The exercise asks you to find the answers to the questions, not to understand all the words in the text.

8 Read

Read the text and (circle) the correct answer: a, b or c.

Hunter "Patch" Adams

When he was a teenager, Hunter Adams was very unhappy, and he spent many years in the 1960s and 1970s in a hospital for people with mental health problems.

When he left the hospital, Adams decided to become a doctor, so he went to medical school in the state of Virginia, in the U.S. There he often did things differently from the doctors and other students. For example, he didn't like the doctors' white coats, so he wore shirts with flowers on them when he visited his patients. He also tried to make them laugh. The doctors at the medical school didn't like Adams because he was too different.

But Adams believed that people in a hospital need more than medicine. He saw that patients were lonely and unhappy. He tried to help them, not just as patients but as people, too. He spent a lot of time with children in the hospital. He often put on a red nose to look like a clown and to make the children laugh.

When he finished medical school and became a doctor, Adams and some other doctors began an organization called the Gesundheit Institute. One of their goals is to build a clinic and teaching center. It will be a place with a different way of working with sick people.

Hunter Adams became famous during the 1980s, and in 1998, Universal Pictures made a successful movie about Adams's life called *Patch Adams*. Robin Williams played Adams. Williams said, "Hunter is a really warm person, who believes that patients need a doctor who's a friend. I enjoyed playing him."

1 Hunter Adams went to Virginia because ...
   a he had mental health problems.
   b he wanted to be a doctor.
   c he did things differently.

2 Adams wore shirts with flowers on them because ...
   a he didn't want to wear a white coat.
   b the doctors didn't like him.
   c it made the patients laugh.

3 Adams thought that many people the in hospital ...
   a didn't need medicine.
   b were unhappy and lonely.
   c weren't nice people.

4 Adams started the Gesundheit Institute ...
   a with other doctors.
   b on his own.
   c with different sick people.

5 Universal Pictures made a movie about Hunter Adams because ...
   a Adams built a successful hospital.
   b Robin Williams was Adams's friend.
   c Adams was a famous person.

Unit check

1 Fill in the blanks

Complete the text with the words in the box.

| funny faces | makes fun | since | made fools | ~~to laugh~~ | time | for | make me | haven't | fun |

I love __to laugh__ , and I like people who [1] _____ laugh, like my best friend, Sarah. I've known her [2] _____ nine years, and she's really great. She loves telling jokes, but she never [3] _____ of other people. On weekends, we usually have a lot of [4] _____ . We often go to the park and have a soda and a good [5] _____ together. But one Sunday, a few weeks ago, we [6] _____ of ourselves! We were sitting under a tree in the park, making [7] _____ for about half an hour. Then we saw that two boys from my class were watching us! We [8] _____ been to the park [9] _____ that Sunday!

| 9 |

2 Choose the correct answers

Circle the correct answer: a, b or c.

1 Jacob is nice. He _____ in my class since December.

   a (has been) b is c was

2 How long _____ this bike?

   a you had b have you c have you had

3 I'm going to see my cousin next week. We _____ each other for two years.

   a don't see b haven't seen c didn't see

4 My parents _____ for 15 years.

   a have been married b have married c are married

5 David _____ with us since last summer.

   a has been b is c was

6 I'm sorry I _____ since we last spoke. I've been so busy!

   a didn't call b haven't called c don't call

7 You must be hungry. You _____ since last night.

   a haven't eaten b didn't eat c hasn't eaten

8 My sister has hated tomato soup _____ she was a child.

   a for b when c since

9 Carol and I _____ e-pals for three years.

   a have been b are c been

| 8 |

3 Vocabulary

Complete the sentences. Use the correct form of *make* or *take*.

1 When you called we __were making__ dinner.

2 I think we need to _____ a plan before we start.

3 We aren't in a hurry, so let's _____ our time and enjoy the trip.

4 When I heard what he said, it _____ me smile.

5 My grandfather _____ his driving test when he was 75!

6 Learning the guitar was difficult at first, but now I'm _____ a lot of progress.

7 If you have a better idea, please feel free to _____ a suggestion!

8 He's interested in other people and _____ friends easily.

9 My sister _____ an interest in her friends. They all like her.

| 8 |

How did you do?

Total: | 25 |

| 😊 | Very good 25 – 20 | 😐 | OK 19 – 16 | 😞 | Review Unit 8 again 15 or less |

9 Disaster!

1 Remember and check

Match the two parts of the sentences. Then check with Exercise 1d on page 59 of the Student's Book.

1 In 2005, New Orleans was hit by
2 Many people left the city, but
3 More than 7,000 were
4 The city was badly damaged, and about
5 Many people lost everything they had

a 1,500 people were killed.
b and the damage was 90 billion dollars.
c a terrible hurricane named Katrina.
d rescued by the police and firefighters.
e 80 percent of the city was flooded.

2 Grammar

★ Past passive

a Complete the sentences with the past participle of the verbs in the box.

> speak   lose   give   ~~see~~   send   break

1 The movie *Gladiator* was __seen__ by more than 100 million people.

2 There was a terrible storm last night. Four windows were _____ in our house.

3 The criminals were caught, and they were _____ to prison.

4 Spanish is _____ as a first language by more than 330 million people around the world last year.

5 Thousands of umbrellas were _____ on the New York City subway last year.

6 My twin sister and I were _____ a DVD player for our birthday this year.

b (Circle) the correct words.

1 Melissa (won) / *was won* first prize for her science project this year.

2 The flood destroyed several houses, but luckily no one *killed* / *was killed*.

3 My bicycle *stole* / *was stolen* last week.

4 Luckily, it *found* / *was found* two days later.

5 Television *didn't invent* / *wasn't invented* until 1946.

6 Twenty years later, the first color TVs *sold* / *were sold*.

c Complete the text with the present passive or past passive form of the verbs in parentheses.

Los Angeles __was built__ on the San Andreas fault, one of the worst places in the world for earthquakes. Every year there are about 10,000 earthquakes in LA. Most of these are very small, and they [1] _____ (not feel), but sometimes a few windows [2] _____ (break). In 1994, the city [3] _____ (hit) by a strong earthquake that measured 6.6 on the Richter scale. Many buildings [4] _____ (damage) by fire, a freeway [5] _____ (destroy) by the earthquake and many people [6] _____ (kill) in their cars. After that earthquake, new building laws [7] _____ (introduce), and today all new houses in the Los Angeles area [8] _____ (build) to survive earthquakes.

d Rewrite the sentences. Use the past passive.

1 They built a new road near my house.

   A new road was built near my house.

2 The ice storm killed thousands of trees.

   ....

   ....

3 Someone left the door open last night.

   ....

   ....

4 They printed all the books on time.

   ....

   ....

5 They closed the main train station yesterday.

   ....

   ....

6 Someone stole all my money.

   ....

   ....

7 The hotel bellhop took my suitcase to my room.

   ....

   ....

e Complete the text. Use the simple past or past passive form of the verbs in parentheses.

SUMATRA

Krakatoa

JAVA

Indian Ocean

INDONESIA has many volcanoes. One of the most famous is Krakatoa, a small island volcano in the sea between Java and Sumatra. On the night of August 26, 1883, Krakatoa _erupted_ (erupt). Here are some facts about the eruption:

1 Before the eruption, Krakatoa was an island of about 47 km^2, and people ^{1} .... (live) there. After the eruption, it was only 16 km^2, and now no one can live there.

2 Before 1883, Krakatoa was one island, but after the eruption, a smaller island ^{2} .... (appear). It ^{3} .... (push) out of the ocean by the force of the explosion. The second island ^{4} .... (give) the name Anak Krakatoa, which means "child of Krakatoa" in Indonesian.

3 Thousands of people ^{5} .... (kill), but we don't know exactly how many.

4 There was also an earthquake under the ocean. It ^{6} .... (produce) a tsunami wave that was almost 15 m high. The wave ^{7} .... (destroy) hundreds of villages.

5 The explosion ^{8} .... (make) a very loud noise. It ^{9} .... (hear) by people in Australia!

6 Millions of tons of volcanic dust ^{10} .... (throw) into the atmosphere. This created some of the most beautiful sunsets the world has ever seen.

7 In 1927, Krakatoa ^{11} .... (produce) some small eruptions. Since then, the island has been quiet. But who knows when the next eruption will be?

3 Pronunciation

✱ Silent consonants

▶ **CD3 T38** Read the sentences and <u>underline</u> the consonants that are not pronounced. Then listen, check and repeat.

1 She <u>k</u>nows the ans<u>w</u>er.
2 I <u>w</u>rote the <u>w</u>rong word.
3 Listen to the rhyme.
4 The firefighters climbed up the tree.
5 They built a castle on an island.

4 Vocabulary

✱ Disasters

a Fill in the crossword.

1 Five hundred million dollars of *damage* was caused by a tsunami in Hawaii in 1960.
2 Katrina was the worst ... to hit the U.S. for a very long time.
3 An ... measuring 9.5 ... hit Chile in 1960.
4 ... can happen when rivers have too much water in them.
5 Many people worked for days to ... the victims from the earthquake.
6 Mount Etna is a famous ... in Italy.
7 A ... bomb makes a cloud shaped like a mushroom.
8 Mount Etna erupted in 2008, but luckily no one was ... .
9 An ... storm can cause power lines to break.
10 A ... is a giant wave, often caused by an underwater earthquake.

b 〔Vocabulary bank〕 Complete the sentences with the words in the box.

| collapse | cracked | ~~set fire~~ | catch on fire |
| starving | on fire | homeless | put out |

1 Someone *set fire* to the factory last night.
2 Look at that smoke! I think the building over there is _____ .
3 Hundreds of houses were destroyed, and many people were _____ .
4 When the weather is hot and dry, trees can _____ .
5 We needed a lot of water to _____ the fire.
6 There isn't enough food, so a lot of people are _____ .
7 That house is very old. I think it's going to _____ soon.
8 Sorry! I dropped the glass. It isn't broken, but it's _____ .

5 Grammar

✱ *a/an, the* or zero article

a Complete the sentences with *a* or *an*.

1 I got ___*a*___ bicycle for Christmas.
2 Can I have _____ orange, please?
3 It's raining. Take _____ umbrella with you.
4 We have _____ English test next week.
5 Is this _____ apple or _____ pear?

b Complete the paragraph with *a, the* or [–] (zero article).

Lately [1] __ robberies have been a problem in our neighborhood. Last night, I heard [2] _____ strange noise outside. [3] _____ noise was coming from our neighbor's yard. I saw two people. They had put [4] _____ ladder against the house. One was climbing [5] _____ ladder. I knew the neighbors weren't home, so I called [6] _____ police. They came very quickly. But the people weren't [7] _____ robbers! They were my neighbors. They forget their keys!

6 Culture in mind

a Write *T* (true) or *F* (false). Then check with the text on page 62 in the Student's Book.

1 The Tuvalu islands in the South Pacific are in danger because of climate change. `T`

2 Geographically speaking, Tuvalu is the smallest country in the world. ☐

3 In the southern summer, the group of islands gets severe hurricanes and rough seas. ☐

4 One day, the Tuvaluans will have to leave their islands because there won't be enough food anymore. ☐

5 New Zealand has agreed to take in 9,000 immigrants per year from Tuvalu. ☐

6 The Australian government won't accept immigrants from Tuvalu. ☐

7 It is not clear where the people of Tuvalu will go when they can't live on their islands anymore. ☐

b Complete the sentences with the words in the box. Put the words into their correct form where necessary.

> threaten   reduce   rising   tiny   source
> ~~uninhabitable~~   refuse   rough

1 Tuvalu might become _uninhabitable_ because of climate change.

2 Geographically speaking, Tuvalu is a _____ country.

3 Tuvalu is frequently hit by hurricanes, which cause storms and _____ seas.

4 Frequent hurricanes have started to _____ life in Tuvalu.

5 _____ sea levels have increased the level of salt in the ground water.

6 Ground water is the only _____ of fresh water for people and farm animals.

7 The government has started a program to _____ Tuvalu's emission of greenhouse gases.

8 The Australian government has _____ to take in Tuvaluan immigrants.

7 Study help

✽ Speaking: how to improve your fluency

For many tests and exams, you will have to speak English. Many students think that the **only** important thing is not to make any mistakes, but this is not true! You are tested on your ability to communicate successfully, and fluency is an important part of communication.

Here are some ideas to help you speak fluently:

● Keep calm, and give yourself time to think. Don't rush!

● Think about the message you want to communicate, not only about the grammar.

● If you make a mistake, don't worry! It's normal to make mistakes, so don't stop or panic.

● If you can't remember how to say a word in English, try to explain the word if you can. For example, if you can't remember the word *kitchen*, say, "The room in the house where I cook."

● It's OK to pause or stop occasionally if you need to think about how to say something. But try not to pause too many times or for too long.

● When you are asked questions, try not to give too many short answers. For example, if someone asks, "Do you have any brothers or sisters?" don't just say, "Yes, I do." or "No, I don't." Give more information. Say, for example, "Yes, I have a sister named Sabrina. She's 12. I also have a brother, Marco. He's 11."

Choose one of the topics below. Think about it for one minute, and then try to talk about it for one minute without stopping. It's better if you can do this with a friend or someone in your family.

● my favorite movie star
● my house
● my best friend
● my favorite stores
● the things I like doing in my free time

Skills in mind

LISTENING TIP

Listening for specific information

It's important to look carefully at the task before the listening starts. You are usually given time to do this.

- Read each question very carefully. What kind of information does the question ask you to find? A date? A time? A name? A place?

- You don't need to understand *everything*. Look at the questions and listen carefully for the answers.

- Look at the listening exercise on this page. What kind of information do you need to answer questions 2–5? You will hear the names of cities and other places in the countries. Do you need to listen for these?

8 Listen

✱ Important earthquakes in history

▶ **CD3 T39** Listen to an interview about important earthquakes in history. Put the information in the correct places in the table.

Japan	Ecuador	China	~~Sicily (Italy)~~	Portugal
~~1693~~	1797	1755	1710	1556
80,000	800,000	~~60,000~~	200,000	40,000

	Country	Year	Number of people killed
1	*Sicily (Italy)*	*1693*	*60,000*
2			
3			
4			
5			

9 Read

a Look at the picture and the title of the text. Can you guess what the story is about? Read the text quickly and answer the questions.

1 What are the names of the two people? ....

2 How far were they from Mount St. Helens? ....

3 What saved them from the cloud of smoke?

....

4 How were they finally rescued?

....

b Read the text again and answer the questions.

1 Why did Bruce and Sue think they were safe?

....

2 Do you think they ever returned to Mount St. Helens after this? Why / why not?

....

THEY THOUGHT THEY WERE SAFE

On Sunday, May 18, 1980, the eruption of Mount St. Helens volcano in the state of Oregon killed 57 people. On that day, Bruce Nelson, 22; his girlfriend, Sue Ruff; and some other friends were camping and fishing on the Green River, 13 miles north of Mount St. Helens. They knew that the volcano was showing signs of an eruption, but they thought they were in a safe area.

On that Sunday morning, they saw a cloud of dark smoke coming toward them. Everything turned black. There was thunder and lightning. Trees started falling around them. "There was so much noise you couldn't hear yourself scream," one of Bruce's friends said later. Suddenly, Bruce and Sue fell into a deep hole made by one of the falling trees. In the end, this saved them because other trees fell over the hole and protected them.

A National Guard helicopter flies over Mount St. Helens.

After the cloud of smoke and ash passed, Bruce and Sue found their friends. Their friends had serious burns, but everyone was able to walk. They started walking out of the area. It was very difficult. There were fallen trees everywhere and two feet of ash on the ground. Finally, at the end of the day, they were rescued by a National Guard helicopter.

Bruce and Sue will never forget that terrible day. Sometimes a sound, like the wind in the trees, or the smell of a fire will bring all the memories back to them.

Unit check

1 Fill in the blanks

Complete the text with the words in the box.

hurricanes destroy ~~disasters~~ the volcano floods lose tsunami earthquakes killed

Disasters happen all the time and in many parts of the world. For example, sometimes people on islands in the South Seas are [1] _____ by [2] _____ .

In California, there are a lot of [3] _____ (the one in San Francisco in 1906 was very strong). An earthquake under [4] _____ sea can cause a [5] _____ , a giant wave that can kill or injure thousands of people.

In some countries, when it rains heavily, there are [6] _____ . Many people [7] _____ their homes.

And lastly, when a [8] _____ like Vesuvius or Krakatoa erupts, it can easily [9] _____ everything nearby.

9

2 Choose the correct answers

(Circle) the correct answer: a, b or c.

1 That house _____ last month.

   a sold   b is sold   c (was sold)

2 My dad's car keys _____ yesterday.

   a are stolen   b was stolen   c were stolen

3 That tower _____ hundreds of years ago.

   a were built   b is built   c was built

4 About 2,000 years ago, the city of Pompeii _____ by a volcano.

   a was destroyed   b is destroyed

   c were destroyed

5 On Sunday, I saw _____ interesting TV program about tsunamis.

   a a   b an   c the

6 My mother rides a motorcycle. It's _____ old Kawasaki.

   a a   b the   c an

7 I got _____ nice new photo album for my birthday this year.

   a a   b an   c the

8 When _____ the Sears Tower built?

   a was built   b was   c is

9 In the flood last month, all the houses by the river _____ .

   a destroying   b are destroyed

   c were destroyed

8

3 Vocabulary

Underline the correct word or words in each sentence.

- All the world's countries should work together to [1] _increase / reduce / rise_ their [2] _emission / situation / immigration_ of greenhouse gases.

- The ocean is an important [3] _course / source / program_ of food for the world's people. A fisherman's work is often dangerous because of [4] _tiny / uninhabitable / rough seas._

- When New Orleans was [5] _built / helped / hit_ by Hurricane Katrina, a lot of houses were badly [6] _rescued / upset / damaged._

- The city of Pompeii was completely [7] _reduced / flooded / destroyed_ by a volcano more than two thousand years ago.

- Hurricane Katrina was one of the biggest [8] _floods / damage / disasters_ in American history.

- The [9] _estimate / damage / research_ to the city cost $90 billion.

8

How did you do?

Total: [ ] **25**

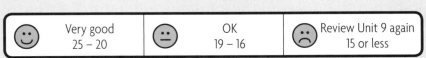

😊	Very good 25 – 20	😐	OK 19 – 16	😞	Review Unit 9 again 15 or less

1 Remember and check

Read part of the text about the historic caves in Andalusia. Put the lines in the correct order. Then check your answers with the text on page 64 of the Student's Book.

	to find everything you need – electricity, phone, hot water. Some caves
	primitive. Well, you haven't seen these caves. A
1	You probably think caves are
	have a Jacuzzi or a swimming pool.
	a small country cottage to a luxurious cave
	even have a broadband connection, and others
	hotel. Come and enjoy the peaceful environment. You'll be surprised
	cave house in Andalusia can be anything from

2 Grammar

★ *too much/many, not enough*

a Use *too much* or *too many* to match the two parts of the sentences.

We spent		tests at school.
Be quiet, please! There's		money today!
I think we get	too much	sugar in my coffee.
Jack was sick because he ate	too many	noise in here.
I put		ice cream yesterday.
You always ask me		questions!

1 *We spent too much money today!* ....

2 ....
....

3 ....
....

4 ....
....

5 ....
....

6 ....
....

b Complete the sentences with *too much*, *too many* or *not (n't) enough*.

1 There were _too many_ people, and there were _n't enough_ chairs for everybody.

There are 50 questions on the test. You have 15 minutes to answer them all.

2 The test was awful! There were .... questions, and there was .... time to answer them all.

3 I think I've made .... food, and there are .... drinks.

4 I've got .... CDs, and there is .... space for them all!

5 The party was awful! There were .... girls and there were .... boys!

3 Pronunciation

* Sound and spelling: -ou-

a ▶ **CD3 T40** Write the words from the lists. Then listen, check and repeat.

enough	~~out~~	famous	could

/aʊ/	/ʌ/	/ʊ/	/ə/
out			

b ▶ **CD3 T41** Say the sentences. Then listen and check.

1 We have a big house.
2 Could I have a glass of water?
3 Those dogs are dangerous.
4 I don't have enough cash!

4 Vocabulary

* Homes

a Look at the picture and write the words in the box in the correct places.

fence	~~window~~	door	yard	garage
chimney	satellite dish			

b Fill in the word puzzle. What's the mystery expression?

1 We have a _satellite_ dish for our TV service.
2 In our new … in the city, we can hear the neighbors on both sides.
3 There's room for two cars in our … .
4 We have a … all around the backyard.
5 In the summer, we like to spend time in our … on the lake.
6 My grandparents live in a nice … home in Florida.
7 You can see the … on the roof of the house.
8 We live in a … -family house with a big yard around it.

1	S	A	T	E	L	L	I	T	E
2					H				
3		A							
4			E						
5						G			
6							L		
7									
8		I							

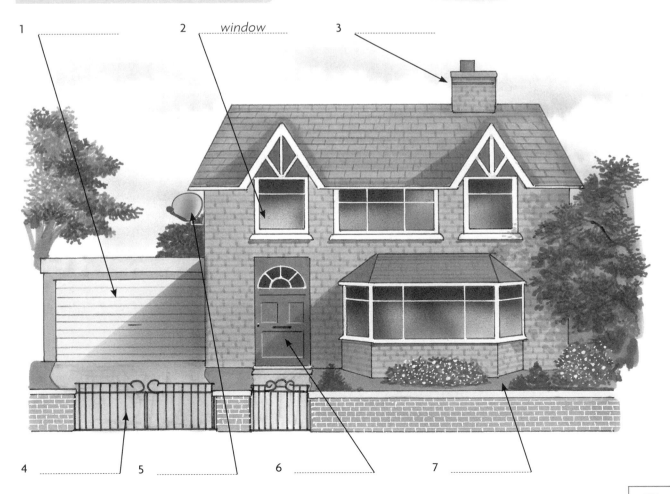

1 _____
2 _window_
3 _____
4 _____
5 _____
6 _____
7 _____

c **Vocabulary bank** Complete the text with the words in the box.

roof   central heating   share   balcony   basement   ~~air conditioning~~   move   attic

Some friends of ours have a cottage at the beach. It's kind of old and doesn't have any _air conditioning_
or ¹_____ (so it's cold in winter!), but it's a great place for weekends. When you go down into
the ²_____ , there are boxes full of old books. I sometimes choose a book, and then I climb
the stairs all the way up to the ³_____ and start reading. It's only a problem when it rains.
The ⁴_____ has a few holes! The house has a ⁵_____ , too, overlooking the
ocean. Unfortunately, my parents want to ⁶_____ , and we're going to live in another city.
It's far away, so we won't be able to visit the cottage so often. And in our new place, I'll have to
⁷_____ a room with my brother! :-(

(5) Grammar

✱ *will* vs. *be going to*

a Underline the correct options. Then
check with the dialogue on page 67 of
the Student's Book.

> Jake is going to ¹ <u>China</u> / *India*.
> He's going to visit a place called
> ² *Beijing* / *Qinghai*, where many
> people still live in a very traditional
> way. He's going to visit some of these
> people in their ³ *tents* / *caravans*. Jake
> will pack some ⁴ *socks* / *warm clothes*
> because it's cold there. When he's
> there, he'll ⁵ *call Marta* / *send Marta*
> *a postcard* if he can.

b Write *A* if the sentence is a decision
made at the moment of speaking, or
B if it's a decision made before the
moment of speaking.

1   I'm bored! I think I'll call Alison. | A |

2   We're going to have a party next
    weekend. | B |

3   Our teacher says he's going to give
    us a test next week. | |

4   I'm hungry. I think I'll make
    a sandwich. | |

5   You don't have any money? Don't
    worry. I'll lend you some. | |

6   It's Steve's birthday next week, and
    I'm going to buy him a great present! | |

7   There's a test next Monday, so I'm
    going to study over the weekend. | |

8   It's very cold in here, isn't it? I'll
    close the window. | |

c Match the sentences with the pictures. Write
1–6 in the boxes.

1   ~~I'll answer it.~~

2   I'll carry it for you.

3   I'm going to New York next month.

4   I'm going to lose weight this year.

5   My dad's going to buy a new one next week.

6   Don't cry. I'll buy you another one.

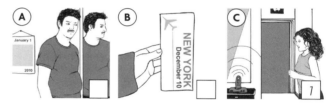

d (Circle) the correct words.

1   I want to visit Paris next year, so I (*'m going to*)
    / *'ll* study French next semester.

2   There aren't any good movies on TV tonight, so
    I think I *'m going to* / *'ll* watch football.

3   My computer's old, so my dad *'s going to* / *'ll* buy
    me a new one for my birthday.

4   My sister and I have planned our vacation.
    We *'re going to* / *'ll* visit our cousin in Canada.

5   I haven't spoken to John for a long time. I think
    I *'m going to* / *'ll* call him now.

6   What can I get Jane for her birthday? I know!
    I *'m going to* / *'ll* take her to the movies.

7   I don't want to do this homework now. I think
    I *'m going to* / *'ll* do it tomorrow instead.

6 Everyday English

a Rewrite each expression. Insert the word in parentheses in the correct place.

1 Anything you need? (else) .... *Anything else you need?* ....

2 If you so. (say) ....

3 It's to you. (up) ....

4 There's point in arguing (no) ....

5 There's nothing with it. (wrong) ....

6 I get. (it) ....

b Complete the dialogues. Use the expressions from Exercise 6a.

1 A: OK. You have skis, boots, poles and warm clothes.
   .... *Anything else you need?* ....

   B: No, I don't think so, thanks.

2 A: This food doesn't look very good. Is it OK to eat?

   B: Yes, it's fine. You can eat it.
   ....

3 A: Look, all you need to do is add 10 and then divide by 2.

   B: Oh, ... now. Thanks for your help.

4 A: Dad, I don't want to go to Aunt Sally's house tomorrow. It's boring!

   B: Listen, Mike. You're coming with us, and that's that. ....

5 A: What should we have for lunch? Pizza or salad?

   B: .... I like them both.

6 A: That new boy, Dan, is really good-looking!

   B: .... , but I don't think he's very special.

7 Study help

✱ Vocabulary: nouns and verbs

a Many nouns don't change form when used as verbs. Study these examples:

● I <u>promise</u> I'll bring the book back tomorrow. (verb)
● I'll call you next week. That's a <u>promise</u>! (noun)

b Look at the <u>underlined</u> words in sentences 1–10 and write *V* (verb) or *N* (noun).

1 We're going to <u>move</u> next month. | *V*

2 Come on, Steve. It's your <u>move</u>. | *N*

3 Are you thirsty? I'll get you some <u>water</u>. | ☐

4 We're going to <u>water</u> the plants now. | ☐

5 My dad's going to <u>work</u> in San Diego next week. | ☐

6 Sorry, I'm busy. I've got too much <u>work</u> to do. | ☐

7 I'm redoing my bedroom, so I need to buy some <u>paint</u>. | ☐

8 I'm going to <u>paint</u> each wall a different color. | ☐

9 Would you like a <u>drink</u> of water? | ☐

10 I usually <u>drink</u> coffee in the morning. | ☐

8 Read

a Read this advertisement for a house and answer the questions.

Single-family home in city

This single-family house was built in the 1940s and is located on a quiet residential street not far from downtown. Schools, transportation and stores are all nearby. The house has been well maintained by the most recent owners.

Downstairs there is a spacious living room with an open fireplace, separate dining room, a large modern kitchen and a utility area with a washer and dryer. Upstairs there are two large bedrooms, plus a master suite and two bathrooms. There is also a yard in the front and back, with trees and garden areas and an attached two-car garage.

Asking price: $300,000.
Any reasonable offer considered.

**For more information or to make an appointment call OurTown Realty,
818-555-6789**

b Write *T* (true) or *F* (false).

1	The house is on a busy street.	F
2	Schools are far away from the house.	
3	The living room is large.	
4	The house has two floors.	
5	The house has no front yard.	
6	The buyer will have to pay $300,000 for the house.	
7	If you want to visit the house, you have to call first.	

READING TIP

Reading for detailed information

Sometimes you need to read part of a text very carefully to answer a question correctly.

- When you read a question, always go to the place in the text where you can find the answer. Read the sentence(s) there two or three times, and compare what you read with the question. The answer can sometimes depend on just one or two words.

- Look at the reading text in Exercise 8, and the *true/false* questions.

  – Look at question 1. Which sentence in the text will tell you the answer? (the first sentence)

  – Which words in the sentence describe the street? (quiet, residential)

  – Is the house in the downtown area or just near it? (near it)

  – What does this tell you about how busy the street probably is?

  – Is question 1 true or false? (false)

Do the same for the other six questions.

9 Write

Write a description of the house or apartment where you live. Include the following information:

- the age of your house/apartment
- the location (the center of the city, a suburb, a small town?)
- things near your house/apartment (schools, stores, movie theaters, parks?)
- the number of rooms in your house/apartment, and a short description of each room
- what you like most about your house/apartment

1 Fill in the blanks

Complete the text with the words in the box.

> floor   log cabin   neighbors   ~~apartment~~   houses   far   yard   two-family   chimney   housing   garage

My dad says that he wants us to move into an ___apartment___ building! But I don't want to move. I like our nice ¹_____ house! We have a ²_____ for the car, and my brother and I can play in the ³_____ here, too. I know it's a little noisy because our ⁴_____ sometimes play loud music, but who wants to live in an apartment? I don't think it's nice to have everything on one ⁵_____ . Also they can't have a fire, because there's no ⁶_____ or fireplace! I don't want to live in a ⁷_____ development either because all the ⁸_____ look the same. I'd really like to live in a ⁹_____ in the country, so I can make as much noise as I want to, but my dad says it's too ¹⁰_____ from his job.

`10`

2 Choose the correct answers

Circle the correct answer: a, b or c.

1 I can't hear you. There's _____ noise.
   a (too much)   b too many   c not enough

2 I have _____ emails to write.
   a too much   b too many   c not enough

3 We don't have _____ food for everybody.
   a enough   b too much   c too many

4 A: I'm so busy!
   B: Don't worry. _____ help you.
   a I'm going to   b I'll   c I

5 On Saturday, we _____ see the Kings of Leon in concert.
   a go to   b 're going to   c 'll

6 They _____ Mexico for three weeks this summer.
   a 're going to   b 'll go to   c go to

7 I don't think there _____ be cars in the future.
   a won't   b aren't going to   c 'll

8 I didn't finish my project because there wasn't _____ information on the Internet.
   a too many   b enough   c too much

9 Next week we _____ U2 live. We've bought the tickets!
   a 're going to see   b 'll see   c see   `8`

3 Vocabulary

The underlined words in this exercise are in the wrong sentences! Cross out the word and write the correct word in the blank.

1 It's getting warm in here. Maybe the ~~gate~~ isn't working. __air conditioning__

2 Don't open the cottage. There's a dog in the yard! _____

3 My grandparents like to sit on the attic of their apartment in the summer.
   _____

4 They're staying at their balcony at the beach for the summer.
   _____

5 It must be great to live in a roof. They're small, but very comfortable.
   _____

6 Wow! That tree fell right on the air conditioning of the house.
   _____

7 We are going to change one room downstairs in the mobile home to a gym. _____

8 I found this book in a box upstairs in our basement. _____   `7`

How did you do?

Total: `25`

😊 Very good 25 – 20	😐 OK 19 – 16	🙁 Review Unit 10 again 15 or less

1 Remember and check

(Circle) the correct information in each sentence. Then check your answers with the text on page 72 of the Student's Book.

1   Your brain is like a muscle. You must (use) / lose it or use / (lose) it.

2   The brain makes up 2 / 20 percent of our total body weight and needs 2 / 20 percent of the oxygen that our body takes in.

3   No one / Everyone can remember everything / nothing, but no one / everyone can learn how to improve their memory.

4   When you want to remember something / somebody, tell something / somebody about it.

5   It's better to study a lot / a small amount of material for a lot / a small amount of time than the other way around.

2 Grammar

✱ Indefinite pronouns (everyone, no one, someone, etc.)

a (Circle) the correct words.

1   This is a great DVD. I think (everyone) / all of them should buy it.

2   There were a lot of questions. Some of them / All of them were easy, but the others were difficult.

3   We always go to the same place! Can't we go everywhere / somewhere different tonight?

4   I've traveled to lots of countries, but somewhere / nowhere is as beautiful as my country.

5   I don't know what to buy Jamie for his birthday. He has everything / everyone!

6   You've eaten all the food! There's nothing / something left!

7   He's a really terrible person! No one / Everyone likes him.

8   I have five brothers and sisters, and no one / none of them likes music!

b Look at the pictures and complete the sentences. Use indefinite pronouns (everyone, no one, someone, etc).

1   I invited a lot of people to my party, but ___everyone___ was late.

2   I have a lot of T-shirts, and _____ are black!

3   I've looked _____ , but I just can't find my camera!

4   I dialed the wrong number. _____ answered, but I didn't know who it was.

5   I have a lot of friends at school, but _____ are as tall as me.

6   The bus was full, and there was _____ to sit.

3 Vocabulary

✻ Thinking

a Fill in the word puzzle.

					R				
					E				
					A				
					L				
					I				
					Z				
					E				

1 I was very tired, so I couldn't ... on my work.
2 I didn't know the answers, so I had to ... .
3 I can't ... what it's like to walk on the moon!
4 That's not true! I don't ... you.
5 I ... it's fun to learn another language.
6 He looked very different. I didn't ... him!
7 It's late, so I ... I should go to bed.

b Complete the sentences with the words in the box.

naturalistic   mathematical   intrapersonal   visual   ~~body~~   verbal   interpersonal   musical

1 Soccer players and dancers usually have a lot of *body* intelligence.

2 People with _____ intelligence are often good at drawing.

3 My friend Mandy would like to have more _____ intelligence!

4 Sometimes even young children have good logical- _____ intelligence.

5 If you enjoy being on your own, you probably have a lot of _____ intelligence.

6 You need _____ intelligence to be a good speaker.

7 It's great to go bird-watching with Peter. He has a lot of _____ intelligence.

8 My brother doesn't have much _____ intelligence.

c (Vocabulary bank) Complete the sentences.

1 My friend called me while I was doing my homework and broke my *concentration* .

2 Her _____ of American history is amazing.

3 He has a fantastic _____ and writes amazing stories.

4 A: Can you give me _____ for the work?
   B: Yes, it will be about $400.

4 Grammar

★ *must / must not / don't have to*

a Complete the sentences with *must* or *must not*.

1 Hurry up, James. We ___must not___ be late!

2 I _____ remember to call Sonia tonight.

3 Here's your present. You _____ open it before your birthday!

4 I've told you before. You _____ play football in the street.

5 You _____ forget to lock the door before you leave.

6 If you go to London, you _____ go to the zoo. It's great!

7 My old dictionary is useless. I _____ buy a new one.

b Match the sentences with the pictures. Write the correct sentence (*i* or *ii*) for each picture.

1

a *ii You don't have to eat it.* b _____

2

a _____ b _____

3

a _____ b _____

4

a _____ b _____

1 i You must not eat it. ~~ii You don't have to eat it.~~
2 i She doesn't have to walk. ii She must not walk.
3 i You must not look! ii You don't have to look!
4 i I must not move! ii I don't have to move.

c (Circle) the correct words.

1 You can borrow it, but you (must not) / *don't have to* break it.

2 No, I'm sorry. You *must not / don't have to* bring your pet into the classroom.

3 It's a secret, OK? You *must not / don't have to* tell anyone else!

4 Wow! He *must not / doesn't have to* jump!

5 Stop! You *must not / don't have to* ride your bikes in the park!

6 I know it's raining, but you *must not / don't have to* wear all that!

d Complete the sentences with *must not* or *don't / doesn't have to*.

1 Be quiet! The baby's asleep, so we _must not_ make any noise.

2 My older sister has a job now, so she _____ ask our parents for an allowance.

3 The homework's easy, so you _____ help me.

4 Don't talk like that, Josh! You _____ be rude to your friends.

5 You _____ borrow my things without asking me!

6 My grandfather's 75, so he _____ pay to travel on the bus.

7 It's a test, so you _____ look at other people's work.

5 Pronunciation

✱ *must not / (don't) have to*

a ▶ **CD3 T42** *Must not* expresses a strong negative feeling. Both words are stressed. Listen and repeat.

1 You must not go out.
2 We must not be late.
3 You must not open it.
4 We must not ask questions.

b ▶ **CD3 T43** In the phrase *don't have to, have to* is pronounced as /hæf tə/. Listen and repeat.

1 I don't have to study hard.
2 You don't have to shout!
3 He doesn't have to go.
4 We don't have to worry.

7 Study help

✱ How to study effectively

6 Culture in mind

Answer the questions about Alia Sabur. Then check with the text on page 76 of the Student's Book.

1 Why wasn't it a surprise that Alia Sabur became the youngest person in history to be a university professor?

Because she had done many other things at a very early age.

2 When did Alia start to read books usually read by older children?

_____ .

3 What sport is Alia good at?

_____ .

4 What sport is she *not* good at?

_____ .

5 How did Alia help the people of New Orleans after Hurricane Katrina?

_____ .

6 Where did she go to teach when she turned 19?

_____ .

An important part of learning something is making sure you plan your time and use it well. If you want to remember things well, you need to review information you've learned. Try to follow this advice:

DO	DON'T
• Make a study schedule at least three weeks before your exams, and allow time to relax and have fun.	• Stay up very late studying the night before an exam. This will make you tired, and your brain won't work well.
• Review a little at a time, but often.	• Study for a long period of time without a break. You probably won't remember information very well if you do this.
• While you're studying, take short, regular breaks. A short break every 45 minutes is a good idea. Stand up and walk around. You'll feel more awake!	• Worry too much. If you feel anxious, you won't learn as well as if you're relaxed.
• Try making a week's plan showing what you do every day (school, travel, meals, etc.). You might see where you're wasting time that you could use to study or read.	

Skills in mind

WRITING TIP

Using linking words

Read the short story below. What did the boy in the story think he forgot? _____

> Yesterday, I was watching television ¹ _____when_____ I suddenly remembered that the next day was my father's birthday.
>
> I put my coat on quickly, and ² _____ I ran outside to catch a bus. ³ _____ I went into a music store, but I couldn't remember which CD my dad wanted. ⁴ _____, I decided to go to the bookstore. I wasn't sure what to get. I stayed there for a long time trying to choose a book. ⁵ _____ , I bought him a book about racing cars.
>
> ⁶ _____ I went home again and told my mom about the present. She looked at me strangely for some time, and ⁷ _____ she said, "But your father's birthday is next month!"

When you are writing a story, you can make it clearer and more interesting by using linking words. Complete the story. Use the linking words in the box. Note that you can use the linking words in different orders.

> then ~~when~~ after that first in the end finally then

8 Listen

a ▶ **CD3 T44** Jane and Mack are talking together. Jane has had a bad day. Listen to their conversation and write numbers 1–5 in the boxes.

b ▶ **CD3 T44** Which of the words in the box in the Writing tip does Jane use in her story? Listen again and check (✓) the words and phrases you hear.

9 Write

Write a story about when you remembered, or forgot, something very important. Use the questions below and the story in the Writing tip to help you.

- When did your story happen?
- Where were you when you remembered or forgot the important thing? What were you doing?
- What exactly did you forget (or remember)?
- What did you do after that?
- What happened in the end?

Write about 100–120 words.

Tony

Unit check

1 Fill in the blanks

Complete the text with the words in the box.

> someone   bad memory   remember   forget   ~~memory~~
> remind   memorize   remembers   some of them   imagine

I think my _memory_ is pretty good. I always [1]_____ people's names, and I mean all the names, not just [2]_____ . When I meet [3]_____ and I hear the person's name, I [4]_____ that I can see the name written on the person's face. That's how I never [5]_____ a name. When I have to [6]_____ things for school, I talk aloud while I look at my notes. My brother says he has a very [7]_____ , and he's right! He never [8]_____ his promises. I always have to [9]_____ him.

| 9 |

2 Choose the correct answers

(Circle) the correct answer: a, b or c.

1 _____ said Peter's sick. I think Justin told me.

  a (Someone) b No one c Everyone

2 He was lying on the ground, but _____ helped him.

  a no one b everyone c everywhere

3 You _____ tell me again. I'll remember this.

  a don't have to b must not c must

4 I think the key is _____ in my room.

  a somewhere b nowhere c everywhere

5 You _____ help me. I can do it myself.

  a must b must not c don't have to

6 Joanna _____ buy a new camera. Her old one is still very good.

  a doesn't have to b must not c must

7 You _____ be noisy. Dad is trying to watch TV.

  a must b don't have to c must not

8 I wrote letters to ten people, but _____ answered.

  a no one b everyone c something

9 You really _____ forget to lock the door before you go out.

  a must b must not c don't have to

| 8 |

3 Vocabulary

Match the two parts of each word or phrase. Then complete the sentences.

~~set~~	wonder
turned	history
absent	belt
graduated	on
black	~~records~~
went	from
in	19
no	minded

1 As a child Alia _set records_ as the youngest student in high school and college.

2 When she _____ , she started teaching at a university in Korea.

3 Alia says she is sometimes a little _____ about things like appointments.

4 Alia _____ college when she was 14 years old.

5 She's good at karate and has earned her _____ .

6 After she finished college, she _____ to graduate school.

7 She is the youngest university professor _____ .

8 It's _____ that her parents think she is a special person.

| 7 |

How did you do?

Total: | 24 |

| ☺ Very good 24 – 20 | ☻ OK 19 – 16 | ☹ Review Unit 11 again 15 or less |

12 Music makers

1 Remember and check

Complete the summary of Carlinhos Brown's story with the words in the box. Then check with the text on page 78 of the Student's Book.

> area   leader   complex
> neighborhood   albums
> percussionists   tin cans
> violence   ~~pop scene~~

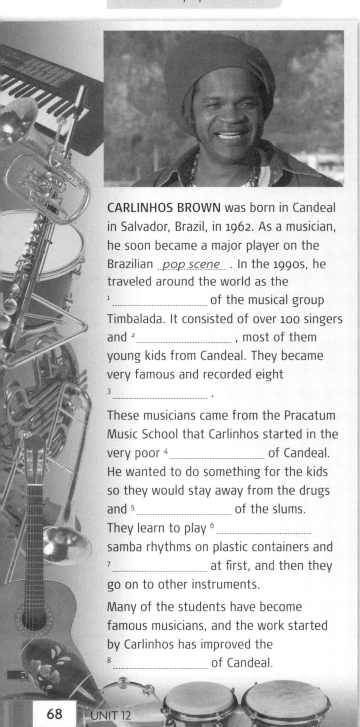

CARLINHOS BROWN was born in Candeal in Salvador, Brazil, in 1962. As a musician, he soon became a major player on the Brazilian _pop scene_ . In the 1990s, he traveled around the world as the
¹ .... of the musical group Timbalada. It consisted of over 100 singers and ² .... , most of them young kids from Candeal. They became very famous and recorded eight
³ ....

These musicians came from the Pracatum Music School that Carlinhos started in the very poor ⁴ .... of Candeal. He wanted to do something for the kids so they would stay away from the drugs and ⁵ .... of the slums. They learn to play ⁶ .... samba rhythms on plastic containers and ⁷ .... at first, and then they go on to other instruments.

Many of the students have become famous musicians, and the work started by Carlinhos has improved the
⁸ .... of Candeal.

2 Grammar

✶ Present perfect continuous

a Match the pictures with the sentences. Write numbers 1–6 in the boxes.

1 You've been sitting there for 20 minutes. What's wrong with you?

2 Where's my cell phone? I've been looking for it all morning!

3 Let's stop and have something to drink. We've been playing for two hours!

4 I've been trying really hard to understand this, but my French isn't good enough.

5 He's been crying since nine o'clock. What can we do?

6 We've been sitting here all morning. Let's go for a walk.

b Complete the dialogues. Use the present perfect continuous form of the verbs in parentheses.

1 **Cathy:** I'm surprised that Paul speaks Spanish.
   Claire: Why? He _'s been studying_ (study) it for years.

2 **Nick:** .... you .... (try) to call me?
   Joanna: Yes, all morning.

3 **James:** There are terrible floods in the south!
   Annie: I'm not surprised. It .... (rain) for 10 days.

4 **Sam:** I .... (clean up) since eight-thirty!
   Chloe: I can help you if you want.

5 **Marek:** Look. Joshua has a digital camera.
   Anika: So what? I .... (use) a digital camera since 2003.

6 **Penny:** Luisa looks really tired! What .... (do)?
   Mark: I think she .... (run).

c Use the words to write sentences. Use the present perfect continuous.

1 Ryan / live / in Chicago / for 10 years
Ryan has been living in Chicago for 10 years.

2 I / work / really hard

....

3 The sun / shine / all day

....

4 She / not study / hard enough

....

5 You / eat / all morning

....

6 you / wait / for a long time

.... ?

7 he / wash / his car

.... ?

3 Grammar

✱ **Present perfect continuous and present perfect**

a Match the pictures with the sentences. Write numbers 1–6 in the boxes.

1 Well, I haven't been feeling well for a week.

2 I've been going to the gym three times a week for a year.

3 No, I've been sitting here for half an hour.

4 Yes, I do, but I've forgotten your name. Sorry.

5 Thanks. My father's been teaching me since I was three.

6 I know. Five people have already told me.

Don't you remember me?   What's wrong with you?

Your T-shirt's dirty.   You're in really good shape!

You're really good!   Have you just gotten home?

b Check (✓) the correct sentence in each pair. Put an X (✗) next to the incorrect sentence.

1 a Maria has had her car for 11 years. ✓

 b Maria has been having her car for 11 years. ✗

2 a I've been meeting your sister three or four times. ☐

 b I've met your sister three or four times. ☐

3 a Jack's playing soccer. He has scored two goals. ☐

 b Jack's playing soccer. He has been scoring two goals. ☐

4 a They've been buying a new house, and they really like it. ☐

 b They've bought a new house, and they really like it. ☐

5 a I've been reading this book for nine days, but I still haven't finished it! ☐

 b I've read this book for nine days, but I still haven't finished it! ☐

6 a Ouch! I've been burning my finger! ☐

 b Ouch! I've burned my finger! ☐

c Complete the sentences. Use the present perfect or present perfect continuous form of the verbs in parentheses.

1 I *'ve met* (meet) three friends this morning.

2 My brother .... always .... (want) to meet your sister.

3 I hope my teacher won't be angry. I .... (forget) my homework.

4 Great! I .... (do) all my homework. Now I can watch TV.

5 She's awful. She .... (talk) about herself all evening.

6 He .... (write) four emails this morning.

7 My father .... (use) the computer since eight o'clock this morning!

8 We .... (clean) our bedroom all morning.

d Read the information about movie star Arnold Schwarzenegger. Then complete the dialogue.

A: Where is he from?

B: He was born in ___Austria___, and he lived there for about [1] _____ years.

A: How long [2] _____ (live) in the U.S.?

B: For more than [3] _____ years.

A: How many movies [4] _____ (make)?

B: More than [5] _____ .

A: How long [6] _____ (be married)?

B: Since 1986.

A: How long [7] _____ (work) with the Special Olympics?

B: For more than 25 years.

ARNOLD SCHWARZENEGGER
born 1947 near Graz in Austria
moved to the U.S. in 1968
married Maria Shriver in 1986
more than 30 movies, including:
The Terminator, Eraser, True Lies
worked with the Special Olympics since 1978

4 Pronunciation

✳ Sentence stress: rhythm

▶ **CD3 T45** Underline the words you think are stressed. Then listen, check and repeat.

1 A: How <u>long</u> have you been <u>waiting</u>?

  B: I've been waiting for three hours!

2 A: Where's she been living?

  B: She's been living in Denver.

3 A: What's he been doing?

  B: He's been looking for a new house.

5 Vocabulary

✳ Music and musical instruments

a Put the letters in the correct order. Then complete the sentences.

1 ___Country___ music is very popular in Nashville, Tennessee. (rcoynut)

2 Mick Jagger is a famous _____ singer. (orkc)

3 _____ is very popular among teens these days. (pih-poh)

4 Yo-Yo Ma plays _____ music. (aascsicll)

5 Which do you prefer, _____ or _____ ? (zajz / gereag)

b Fill in the crossword.

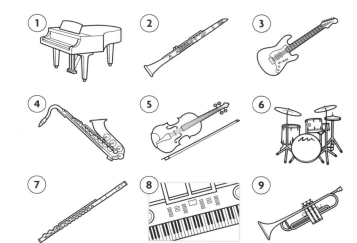

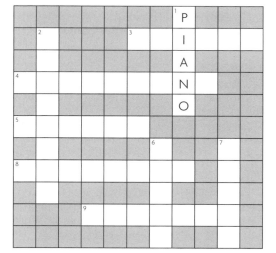

c Circle the correct words.

1 I love the first song on the latest Duffy (album) / single.

2 Oh, no! I left my *stereo / MP3 player* on the bus this morning.

3 I love listening to *live / recorded* music. It's great to see the bands play in person.

4 My parents are buying a new *stereo / personal stereo* for our living room.

5 I never buy *albums/singles* if I only want one song. They're too expensive.

d **Vocabulary bank** Write the words for the definitions.

1 the words of a song *lyrics*

2 a large group of musicians

....

3 the person who directs the performance of musicians ....

4 the place where recordings are made

....

5 a group of singers ....

6 a concert that takes place in a park or a stadium ....

7 Study help

✱ Vocabulary: knowing a word

When you record vocabulary in your notebook, it's important to record more than just the meaning of the word. It might also be a good idea to record these things:

a the pronunciation, including the main stress

b the part of speech (noun, verb, etc.)

c other words that are often used with the new word (For example, if it is a noun, what verbs are used with it?)

d an example sentence (You'll need to know how to use it!)

e any spelling problems (Note things like silent letters or unusual spellings of certain sounds.)

Look at examples 1–5. Match them with one of the tips a–e above.

1 an effort: <u>to make an effort</u>   `c`

2 <u>live</u> music (adj.)   ☐

3 saxo<u>ph</u>one ("f" sound spelled "ph")   ☐

4 enough: /ɪˈnʌf/   ☐

5 musical instrument: I'd like to learn how to play a <u>musical instrument</u>.   ☐

6 Everyday English

Complete the dialogues. Use the expressions in the box.

I'm just saying that   Check it out   ~~I have to say~~   has nothing to do with   What do you mean   loads of

1 A: Do you like my tattoo?

   B: Uh, well, no, not very much. ..*I have to say*.. I don't really like tattoos.

2 A: I'm hungry. Let's get a pizza.

   B: OK. We can go to the mall. There are .... good places there.

3 A: Have you heard any good music recently?

   B: Yes, I have. There's this new CD by Kaiser Chiefs. .... I think you'll like it!

4 A: Don't go to that café. The Bakehouse is nicer.

   B: Oh? Is that café really bad, then?

   A: No, ... there are better places to go.

5 A: I'm surprised that you're wearing a yellow dress.

   B: .... ?

   A: Just that you look better in other colors!

6 A: Oh, are you reading a letter? Who wrote it? Your boyfriend?

   B: Oh, Pauline, go away! It .... you, OK?

Skills in mind

READING TIP

Matching descriptions

In some tests and examinations (for example in PET), you have to read a text and match things. Do this:

- First, read the descriptions of the people carefully because there are clues about the kinds of things they like. Read the description of Carol Morgan in Exercise 8. From this description, we know that she really likes jazz music and that she doesn't like piano music.

- Next, read the book, movie or music descriptions. Remember: You don't need to understand every word. Just look for ideas that go with the people. Read the descriptions in Exercise 8 quickly. We know that Carol Morgan likes jazz music. Which two CDs are jazz? Read those descriptions again. We know Carol doesn't like piano music, so which CD is best for her?

- There will usually be more books, movies or music than people, so be careful!

This week's NEW MUSIC RELEASES

1 The Best of Keith Jarrett
The maestro of jazz piano continues to astound audiences around the world. This collection of his greatest work includes The Köln Concert, Part 1 and extracts from the Paris Concert as well. Excellent value and a must for all jazz lovers. $18.99

2 Richard Thompson 1985–2005
Thompson's stunning electric guitar playing, and his folk-rock songs, are gathered together on a 2-CD collection that shows the best of his work over the last two decades. $26.99

3 Richard Clayderman
French pianist, known for his relaxing piano music, has this new collection out on CD. Ideal as a present for the person who likes relaxing background music. $14.99

4 The Monteverdi Vespers of 1610
This new recording of Monteverdi's great choral work is excellent, with great singing from the Milton Keynes Chorus. Classical music lovers will want to add this one to their collections. $36.99 for the 2-CD set

5 The Best of Paco Peña
The great classical guitarist shows all his brilliance in this new collection. Works by Vila-Lobos and Haydn, among others. Great value at only $14.99

6 Wynton Marsalis
The great jazz trumpeter has put together some of his best-known numbers and a few new pieces on this magical set. Perhaps not as classy as his last offering, but all jazz aficionados will want this one anyway. $20.99

8 Read

The people below all want to buy a CD. Read the descriptions of six CDs and decide which one is right for each person. Write the number of the CD in the boxes.

a Carol Morgan likes many kinds of music, but her favorite is jazz. The only music she doesn't like is piano music, even if it's jazz. `6`

b Mark Moloney doesn't care very much about music, but he likes to have soft, gentle music playing in his apartment sometimes. He isn't very interested in classical or jazz music, but he likes piano playing.

c Andrea Bolton likes all kinds of music, but her favorite instrument is the electric guitar. She's a big fan of John Mayer, for example. She also likes folk music.

d Dave Stone only likes instrumental music. He never buys anything vocal. He likes rock and pop, but his preference is for classical music.

9 Write

Write a text about a CD that you have bought recently and really like. Say:

- who the CD is by and what it is called
- why you decided to buy it
- what kind of music is on the CD
- which songs/tracks are your favorites and why
- how it compares to other CDs in your collection

Unit check

1 Fill in the blanks

Complete the text with the words in the box.

> singer   drums   saxophone   listen   ~~classical~~   plays
> have been playing   has been collecting   has collected   jazz

My father loves *classical* music. He ¹_____ recordings of Mozart's music for 15 years, and I think he ²_____ over 300 so far! My mother was a ³_____ when she was younger, but now she prefers to ⁴_____ to music. My cousins, Cameron and Nicole, ⁵_____ in a band for three years. Nicole ⁶_____ the guitar (she's really good) and Cameron sings. What about me? Well, two years ago my parents bought me some ⁷_____ , and now I am in a ⁸_____ band with three friends from school. My friend, Caleb, is a great ⁹_____ player!

| 9 |

2 Choose the correct answers

(Circle) the correct answer: a, b or c.

1 I'm tired. I _____ for ten hours.
  a ('ve been working)   b 've worked   c work

2 They're angry. They _____ for a very long time.
  a are waiting   b waited   c 've been waiting

3 Tasha _____ six books by John Grisham.
  a has been reading   b have read   c has read

4 How long _____ ? The park is flooded!
  a is it raining   b has it been raining
  c was it raining

5 David _____ in a band since 2001.
  a is playing   b has been playing   c plays

6 Look! Someone _____ that window.
  a have broken   b has broken
  c has been breaking

7 We _____ Caitlin for years.
  a 've been knowing   b know   c 've known

8 There's a new movie at the Plaza Cinema. _____ it?
  a Do you see   b Have you been seeing
  c Have you seen

9 She _____ on the phone for an hour!
  a 's talking   b 's been talking   c talk

| 8 |

3 Vocabulary

Write the words under the pictures.

1 *drums*

2 _____

3 _____

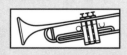

4 _____

5 _____

6 _____

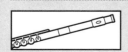

7 _____

8 _____

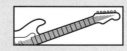

9 _____

| 8 |

How did you do?

Total: | 25 |

| Very good 25 – 20 | OK 19 – 16 | Review Unit 12 again 15 or less |

13 A visit to the doctor

1 Vocabulary

✱ Medicine

a Complete the sentences with the words in the box.

> health   epidemic   hospital   ~~ambulance~~   hurts   shot
> painful   patients   pill   treat   antiseptic

1 There was an accident downtown yesterday. I saw the __ambulance__ arriving.

2 My sister's a nurse. She works at the _____ in town.

3 When the dentist pulled my tooth, it was quite _____ .

4 You shouldn't eat candy. It's bad for your _____ .

5 I went to the doctor yesterday. I had to wait a long time because there were a lot of other _____ .

6 Before the doctor gives you the _____ , she'll clean your skin with some _____ .

7 Some people take a _____ , an aspirin, for example, for a headache.

8 I had a bad stomachache, so I took some medicine to _____ it.

9 I fell down when I was playing tennis, and now my ankle really _____ !

10 Hundreds of people got sick during the flu _____ .

b **Vocabulary bank** Match the sentences.

1 Why does James have a bandage on his hand?
2 Have you taken your temperature?
3 Why is your aunt in a wheelchair?
4 Why doesn't your sister eat yogurt?
5 Is Jane coming to the meeting?
6 How are you doing with your leg in a cast?

a Yes, it's 36.5°. Everything's perfectly normal.
b She's allergic to dairy products.
c No, she can't. She's come down with the flu.
d He cut himself when he broke a window.
e Well, it's not easy to be on crutches!
f She fell out of a tree years ago. She can't walk.

c Complete the sentences with the words in the box.

> hurt   pain   sore   surgeon   stomachache   temperature   ~~toothache~~   vaccination

1 I have a __toothache__ .

2 Oh, that's better! My feet really _____ .

3 Jack feels sick, so his mom's taking his _____ .

4 I ate too much at lunchtime, and now I have a _____ .

5 I have a bad cold and a very _____ throat.

6 I have a _____ in my arm.

7 Don't worry about the operation. The _____ is one of the best in the country.

8 At school, they gave us all a _____ so we wouldn't get the flu this winter.

2 Grammar

✱ Defining relative clauses

a (Circle) the correct words.

1 My mother loves New York. It's the city (*where*) / *that* she was born.

2 There's Jim. He's the boy *whose* / *who* had a party last weekend.

3 Last night, there was a dog *that* / *who* was making a lot of noise under my window.

4 The mall is the place *who* / *where* I meet my friends on the weekend.

5 Don't go to that dentist! He's the one *where* /*who* never smiles!

6 That's the woman *who* / *whose* daughter won the music award.

7 I'll never forget the day *when* / *where* I first met Paul.

b Complete the sentences with *who, that, when, where* or *whose*. Sometimes there is more than one correct answer.

1 Alberto Santos Dumont was a Brazilian _who_ designed planes and balloons.

2 In 1897, he went to Paris, the city .... he made his first flight in a balloon.

3 In 1909, he built a small plane .... was called The Grasshopper.

4 There is an airport in Rio de Janeiro .... is named after him.

5 Martin Luther King Jr. was a man .... goal was to make life better for African Americans in the U.S.

6 The year 1963 was .... he made his famous "I have a dream" speech.

7 Memphis is the city .... King was killed in 1968.

8 The man .... shot Martin Luther King Jr. was James Earl Ray.

c Match the two parts of the sentences. Then write them with a correct relative pronoun.

1 Usain Bolt was the man
2 Andalusia is a place in Spain
3 Lyon is a city in France
4 Evaporation is a process
5 "Crocodile Nests" are huts
6 Pompeii is the city

a you can spend a vacation in a cave.
b puts water back into the atmosphere.
c started a free bicycle program many years ago.
d was destroyed in the year 79 AD.
e set a world record for the 200-meter sprint at the Olympics.
f are used in a ceremony in Papua New Guinea.

1 *Usain Bolt was the man who set a world record for the 200-meter sprint at the Olympics.*

2 ....

3 ....

4 ....

5 ....

6 ....

3 Grammar

✱ used to

a Make sentences or questions with *use(d) to.*

1 I / not play / a lot of volleyball
I didn't use to play a lot of volleyball.

2 we / go/to that park
....

3 that store /be/very cheap
....

4 your father / play / the guitar in a rock band
....

5 my brother / not get / good grades in math
....

6 the Smiths / live / in Toronto
....

b Complete the sentences. Use the correct form of the verb in parentheses in the simple present or *used to*.

1   I _didn't use to have_ (not have) a cell phone, but now I _send_ (send) text messages every day.

2   I _____ (like) potato chips, but now I _____ (eat) fruit and salad.

3   We _____ (not play) tennis now, but we _____ (play) it every day.

4   There _____ (be) three movie theaters in our town, but now there _____ (be) only one.

5   We _____ (not go) on vacation when I was young, but now we _____ (go) to Hawaii every year.

6   My sister _____ (love) rock music, but she _____ (hate) it when she was younger.

7   I _____ (not read) books when I was a child, but now I _____ (read) four every week!

8   A: _____ you _____ (go) to bed early when you were a child?

    B: Yes, I did, but now I _____ (stay) up as late as I want!

c Look at the pairs of pictures and write a sentence for each pair.

How Anna has changed!

Before   After

1   Anna used to _eat potato chips, but now she_ _eats salad._

Before   After

2   Anna used to go _____ _____ .

Before   After

3   Anna _____ _____ .

Before   After

4   Anna _____ _____ .

Before   After

5   Anna _____ _____ .

Before   After

6   Anna _____ _____ .

d Write true sentences about you and your friends or family. Use *used to* or *didn't use to* and the ideas in the box.

music   sports   food   TV   school   home   family

I used to play the piano, but now I play the guitar. My sister ...

_____

_____

_____

4 Pronunciation

★ /z/ or /s/ in *used*

a ▶ **CD3 T46** Listen to the verb *use* in these sentences. ⟨Circle⟩ it when it has a /s/ sound. <u>Underline</u> it when it has a /z/ sound.

1 We <u>used</u> the Internet to find the information.
2 I used to go to bed early when I was young.
3 Who used my MP3 player?
4 My dad used to work in an office.
5 Did he use to play tennis?
6 Did she use my bike?

b ▶ **CD3 T46** Do you hear the *d* in the word *used*? Listen, check and repeat.

5 Culture in mind

Put the lines in order to make a summary of the text "Doctors Without Borders."
Then check with the text on page 90 of the Student's Book.

☐	almost 60 different countries. The organization has helped
☐	and women who work for the organization.
☐	victims in disaster situations in many countries
☐	kidnapped or killed. In 1999, Doctors Without Borders won the Nobel
1	Doctors Without Borders is a non-political
☐	all over the world – in earthquakes, famines or wars.
☐	organization with its headquarters in Geneva,
☐	Peace Prize. The prize honors the courage of the men
☐	Switzerland. It has about 3,000 volunteer doctors in
☐	volunteers. They are sometimes attacked,
☐	Working for Doctors Without Borders is often very dangerous for the

6 Study help

★ Using the Internet

The Internet is a great way for you to practice and use your English! Here are some ideas:

- Visit websites for people who are learning English, with exercises for grammar and vocabulary, and interesting reading and listening texts.
- Find websites in English that have information about things you're interested in: for example, sports, movies and music.
- You can usually copy articles and save them on your computer. Sometimes there are also interviews you can listen to if you want to practice your listening skills. You can also download podcasts from the radio.
- Be careful! Many websites from non-English-speaking countries have versions in English. Sometimes it's good English, but not always! It's often safer if you go to websites from the many English-speaking countries in the world, such as the U.S., Great Britain, Canada.

Skills in mind

7 Listen

▶ **CD3 T47** Listen to six short recordings and (circle) the correct answers.

1. Where are these people?
   a at a bus stop   b (in an airport)   c in a restaurant

2. Who are the people talking?
   a strangers   b child and parent   c friends at school

3. Where are these people?
   a in a store   b on a train   c in a library

4. Who are the people talking?
   a strangers   b child and parent   c friends at school

5. Where are these people?
   a in a plane   b in a restaurant   c in a car

6. Who are the people talking?
   a teacher and student
   b mother and daughter   c friends at school

LISTENING TIP

Identifying places and speakers

When you listen to recordings, you often need to identify where, or who, the people are. On some tests you listen to a recording, and choose from three or four possible answers.

- Always listen to the whole recording. **Never** choose your answer before the recording has finished.

- Look at **Exercise 7 question 1**, for example. You'll hear someone say that she missed the bus, so you might think it's a bus stop. But be careful! The other person later says, "The plane's delayed," and finally, he says, "before we **check in** for our **flight**," so what's the correct answer?

8 Read

a Who is the man in the photo? Why do you think he is famous? Read the text quickly to find the answers.

Christiaan Barnard

These days, people with severe heart problems can have a heart transplant. In other words, another heart is put into their body to replace the heart with problems.

Christiaan Barnard was the surgeon who performed the first human heart-transplant operation. Barnard was born in 1922, in South Africa. He studied medicine at the University of Cape Town and graduated in 1953. Then he went to the United States and studied at the University of Minnesota. He returned to the University of Cape Town in 1958 to teach surgery. No one knew very much about him, but in 1967 he became world famous.

On December 3, Barnard transferred the heart of a 25-year-old woman into the body of Louis Washkansky, a 55-year-old grocer. Unfortunately, Washkansky died 18 days later. Barnard did a second transplant, on January 2, 1968, for a man named Philip Blaiberg. This one was a lot more successful, as Blaiberg lived for more than 18 months after the operation.

Barnard was not the usual picture of a surgeon. Young and handsome, he spent as much time in nightclubs as he did in operating rooms. He met the Pope in Rome and President Lyndon Johnson in the U.S. He knew many beautiful movie stars of the time, like Sophia Loren. However, he was also a dedicated doctor and performed free surgery on hundreds of very sick people.

He died in September 2001, aged 78.

b Read the text again and answer the questions.

1. What nationality was Christiaan Barnard?

   He was South African.

2. In which two countries did he study?

3. When did he become famous?

4. Who was the first person to get a heart transplant?

5. How long did Philip Blaiberg live after his heart transplant?

6. In what ways was Barnard different from other surgeons?

Unit check

1 Fill in the blanks

Complete the text with the words in the box.

| hurts | who | sore throat | treat | ended up with |
| temperature | ~~health problems~~ | pain | ambulance | that |

I never usually have _health problems_ , but two days ago, I had to study for my math test. After five hours, I ¹_____ a toothache! My dad took me to see a dentist, ²_____ said the real problem was a "complete unwillingness to study." Anyway, I didn't take the test, so I have to take it tomorrow. Right now, I'm in bed. I'm really hot. I think I have a ³_____ of about 100°, and I have a really bad ⁴_____ , so I can hardly talk. A minute ago, I wanted to take a pill to stop the ⁵_____ , so I got out of bed and tripped over some math books ⁶_____ were on the floor. Now I can't stand up because my ankle ⁷_____ ! I think Dad should call an ⁸_____ to take me to the hospital. I'm sure the doctors there will know how to ⁹_____ me!

| 9 |

2 Choose the correct answers

Circle the correct answer: a, b or c.

1 I'd like to live in a place _____ the sun shines all the time.

a who b that c **where**

2 Your doctor can give you a pill _____ will stop the pain.

a where b who c that

3 He's the director _____ last movie won an Oscar.

a that b whose c where

4 The jeans _____ were in the window were really expensive.

a where b who c that

5 The people _____ saw the game were lucky.

a where b whose c who

6 Is June the month _____ school ends?

a who b when c where

7 Did you _____ to like going to the dentist?

a used b use c not

8 In the past, people _____ illnesses with strange methods.

a used b used to treat c use to treat

9 We _____ enjoy running, but now we love it!

a usedn't to b didn't use to c used to not

| 8 |

3 Vocabulary

Complete the sentences with the correct words in each group.

| vaccination | pill | ~~epidemic~~ |

1 The disease affected so many people that it became a true _epidemic_ .

2 To make sure you don't get the flu again, why don't you have a flu _____ .

3 I wasn't getting better, so the doctor gave me a vitamin _____ .

| patient | surgeon | ambulance |

4 Claire had a bad accident, and the _____ had to operate on her for hours.

5 My aunt is a doctor. Right now, she's visiting a sick _____ in the hospital.

6 The _____ arrived only a few minutes after the accident.

| chest | stomachache | antiseptic |

7 I drank a lot of cold fruit juice and got a bad _____ .

8 My dad was treated for heart problems because he had a pain in his _____ .

9 A: Look, I've cut my finger. B: You should put some _____ on it.

| 8 |

How did you do?

Total: | 25 |

|  | Very good 25 – 20 | | OK 19 – 16 |  | Review Unit 13 again 15 or less |

14 If I had ...

1 Remember and check

There is one mistake in each sentence. <u>Underline</u> it and write the correct answer.
Then check with the text on page 92 of the Student's Book.

1 Kylie has her own <u>web page</u> on myspace.com. ....*blog*....

2 Brett frequently posts blogs. ....

3 Kylie hates a website called agirlsworld.com. ....

4 Kylie sometimes sends her own designs to podcasts. ....

5 Brett prefers videocasts to websites. ....

6 Brett would love to work as a computer programmer. ....

2 Grammar

✱ Second conditional

a Match the pictures with the
sentences. Write 1–6 in the boxes.

1 If I were taller, I'd get it and eat it.

2 If I had enough money, I'd live in a hot,
dry country.

3 If I had a bicycle, I wouldn't walk to
school anymore.

4 If we didn't have so much homework,
we'd go to the beach.

5 I'd see that movie if I were older.

6 We'd win more games if we were
taller.

b Circle the correct words.

1 If we *had* / *would have* a bigger
house, I *had* / *'d have* my own
bedroom.

2 If I *had* / *'d have* more money, I *went*
/ *'d go* and visit my uncle in France.

3 If we *didn't* / *wouldn't* have to walk
the dog, we *didn't* / *wouldn't* get as
much exercise.

4 I *liked* / *'d like* our town more if there
were / *would be* more places for
teenagers.

5 I *bought* / *'d buy* a DVD player if they
weren't / *wouldn't be* so expensive.

6 We *went* / *'d go* out if we *didn't* /
wouldn't have so much homework.

c Complete the sentences. Use the correct form
of the verbs in parentheses.

1 If I ....*were*.... (be) older, I'd be able to drive.

2 If my brother .... (leave) home,
I .... (have) his bedroom.

3 If I .... (know) the answers,
I .... (tell) you!

4 Your parents .... (be) angry if they
.... (know) what you've done.

5 If we .... (not have) a TV,
.... you .... (read)
more books?

6 If Lou .... (not know) how to
dance, she .... (not enter) the salsa
contest.

d Write the sentences using the second conditional.

1 I don't have a bicycle, so I walk to school.
   If I had a bicycle, I wouldn't walk to school.

2 We don't have a computer, so we don't send emails.
   ....

3 I love music, so I spend all my money on CDs.
   ....

4 I'm not a good athlete, so I'm not on the school team.
   ....

5 I do a lot of exercise, so I'm in good shape.
   ....

6 My uncle speaks good Spanish, so he watches Mexican TV programs.
   ....

e Write true sentences about you or people you know. Use your own ideas or the ideas in the box.

school
money
sports
travel
computers
friends and family

If I didn't have so much homework, I'd go out every night.
....
....
....
....

✱ Giving advice

f Match the problems with the possible advice.

1 I have a terrible headache!
2 I'm bored!
3 It's cold in here!
4 I find the grammar very hard!
5 I need information for my project!
6 My eyesight's bad. I can't read the board!

a If I were you, I'd close the window.
b I'd talk to the teacher if I were you.
c If I were you, I'd get some glasses.
d If I were you, I'd take an aspirin.
e I'd play a computer game if I were you.
f If I were you, I'd search the Internet.

g Write some advice for the people in the pictures. Use the second conditional.

1 *If I were you, I'd go to the dentist.*

2 ....
   ....

3 ....
   ....

4 ....
   ....

5 ....
   ....

6 ....
   ....

(1) I have a toothache!

(2) I'm so tired!

(3) I'm really, really hungry!

(4) I have a big problem at school!

(5) I can't sleep!

(6) I don't understand this! $(ax^2 + bx + c = 0)$

3 Vocabulary

★ Information technology and computers

a Complete the text with the words in the box.

> run ~~logged on~~ touch pad surf printer password memory stick
> download keyboard hard drive crashed saved screen

It was so strange the other day. I had just _logged on_ to my laptop to ¹_____ the web for a while when I suddenly heard this noise. I could also see some color changes on the ²_____ , so I got a little worried. I checked the ³_____ , and it was OK. I could type without any problems. I turned on the ⁴_____ . It worked fine, in color and in black and white. I checked the mouse and the ⁵_____ , and everything was OK. Then I called a friend. She suggested I should ⁶_____ a virus scanning software. I managed to ⁷_____ one for free. When I wanted to key in the ⁸_____ , a message said "There's a problem with your ⁹_____ ." I panicked and ¹⁰_____ my most important files on a ¹¹_____ .

Then my laptop shut down. The hard drive ¹²_____ ! Now I don't know if I should call myself lucky or unlucky!

b Complete the words.

1 I spend a lot of time online in c _h_ _a_ t r o _o_ _m_ _s_.

2 I need to get a battery c __ __ __ g __ r because I'm taking my laptop on a business trip.

3 When you look for something on the web, which __ e __ r __ h __ n __ __ ne do you use?

4 There was a problem with my Internet connection last night, and I was __ __ f __ i n __ for hours.

5 Some new laptops don't have a CD __ __ i __ __ anymore.

6 I can't turn on my computer. There's a problem with the p __ w __ __ __ o r __ .

c (Vocabulary bank) Look at the pictures and fill in the word puzzle.

What's the mystery word? _____

4 Pronunciation

✱ 'd

a ▶ **CD3 T48** Listen and (circle) the words you hear.

1 *I open /* (*I'd open*) *the window.*

2 *They eat / They'd eat meat.*

3 *I ask / I'd ask the teacher a lot of questions.*

4 *We love / We'd love tuna sandwiches for lunch.*

5 *They listen / They'd listen to music.*

6 *We have / We'd have a really good time.*

b ▶ **CD3 T48** Listen again and repeat the sentences.

5 Everyday English

a Complete the expressions. Use the words in the box.

good—like   same   shame   show   worth

1 Looks ____*like*____   4 at the _____ time

2 It's a _____   5 It's not _____ it

3 It's no _____   6 It just goes to _____

b Complete the dialogues. Use the expressions from Exercise 5a.

1 A: Hey! Try one of these new cookies.
     They're delicious, and __*at the same time*__ , they're
     good for you!

   B: OK. Let me try one. Ugh! It's horrible.

   A: But it's good for you!

   B: ¹ _____ . I can't eat it.

   A: Well, ² _____ you that some people
      don't understand good food!

2 A: Hey, look! The Lamas are playing a concert
      here next month! But look
      at the price.

   B: Yeah. They're a really good
      band, but $80?
      ³ _____ .

   A: ⁴ _____ we
      aren't going to the concert.

   B: That's right.
      ⁵ _____ , though.
      I like them a lot.

6 Study help

✱ How to give a good presentation

You may have to give a presentation in English at school, for a test or in your future job. Here are some tips:

- Find the information you need for your talk well before the day of the presentation. You can find a lot of information in libraries or on the Internet.

- Make notes. Write down the most important words. You don't need to write sentences because it isn't usually a good idea to read aloud. A good speaker will look at the audience, not at his or her notes.

- Make sure your presentation has a good, interesting start and ending. This is what your audience will remember most.

- Find pictures, diagrams, graphs and so on to show your audience if you can. This always helps listeners to enjoy a talk and listen carefully.

- Some time before your presentation, ideally the day before, practice what you are going to say. You can do this alone, of course. If there is a time limit, time yourself to make sure your talk isn't too long or too short.

- Before you begin your talk, try not to feel nervous. It's a good idea to try relaxation exercises, for example deep breathing and positive thinking!

7 Read

Read the text and (circle) the correct answer: a, b, c or d.

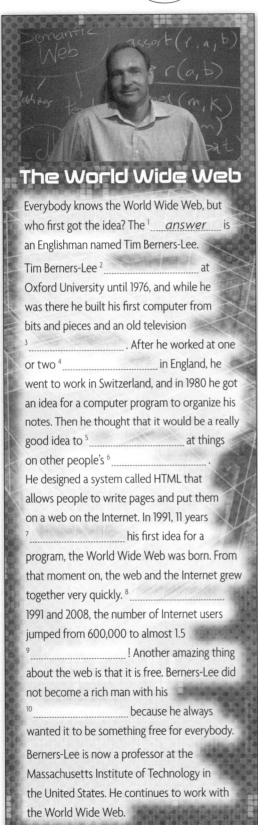

The World Wide Web

Everybody knows the World Wide Web, but who first got the idea? The [1] _____answer_____ is an Englishman named Tim Berners-Lee.
Tim Berners-Lee [2] _____ at Oxford University until 1976, and while he was there he built his first computer from bits and pieces and an old television [3] _____. After he worked at one or two [4] _____ in England, he went to work in Switzerland, and in 1980 he got an idea for a computer program to organize his notes. Then he thought that it would be a really good idea to [5] _____ at things on other people's [6] _____.
He designed a system called HTML that allows people to write pages and put them on a web on the Internet. In 1991, 11 years [7] _____ his first idea for a program, the World Wide Web was born. From that moment on, the web and the Internet grew together very quickly. [8] _____ 1991 and 2008, the number of Internet users jumped from 600,000 to almost 1.5 [9] _____! Another amazing thing about the web is that it is free. Berners-Lee did not become a rich man with his [10] _____ because he always wanted it to be something free for everybody.
Berners-Lee is now a professor at the Massachusetts Institute of Technology in the United States. He continues to work with the World Wide Web.

1	a idea	b (answer)	c name	d question
2	a studied	b went	c wanted	d did
3	a movie	b set	c program	d channel
4	a televisions	b jobs	c works	d companies
5	a look	b see	c read	d listen
6	a books	b webs	c computers	d televisions
7	a before	b when	c after	d until
8	a As	b To	c From	d Between
9	a billion	b thousand	c users	d more
10	a money	b discovery	c Internet	d invention

READING TIP

Multiple choice cloze texts

On many exams (for example, PET) you read a text with blanks and choose words to fill in the blanks. It tests your vocabulary and grammar. Remember:

- Read the complete text first, before you answer the questions. You can't do the exercise well if you don't understand the whole text, and sometimes the information you need is after the blank.

- Read all the possible answers carefully. Sometimes one or more answers are clearly wrong. Identify them first and put a line through them. Look at **Exercise 7**. In number 1, *d* (*question*) is clearly wrong, so put a line through it.

- Read the words before and after the blank before you choose your answer. For example, in **Exercise 7**, the sentence before blank number 1 is a question, so the correct answer is *b* (*answer*). In number 2, *b* (*went*) is not the correct answer, because the word after the blank is *at*, and people say *went/go to*, not *went at*.

8 Write

Write a paragraph about how the Internet has changed people's lives since 1991. Use these questions:

- What do you and people you know use the Internet for?
- How do you think people did these things before 1991?
- Do you think there are things you can do on the Internet that people couldn't do at all in the past?
- Do you think the Internet and web have improved people's lives? Why / Why not?

Unit check

1 Fill in the blanks

Complete the text with the words in the box.

| crashes | didn't | downloads | Internet | screen | had | logs on | ~~computer~~ | printer | search |

My father is a journalist, and he uses an old _computer_ to write. He doesn't take a ¹ _____ with him when he travels. He just looks at the text on the ² _____ , corrects it and then ³ _____ to the internet and sends the text to his newspaper. He also uses the ⁴ _____ when he wants to ⁵ _____ for information. When he ⁶ _____ files, he always burns a CD so that he has copies. His computer isn't very good, and it often ⁷ _____ . He says that if he ⁸ _____ enough money, he'd buy a better computer. My mother says that he'd have more money if he ⁹ _____ spend it so quickly!

9

2 Choose the correct answers

Ⓒircle the correct answer: a, b or c.

1 Claire would find a lot of information if she _____ on the Internet.

   a looks   b would look   c ⓛooked

2 I wouldn't do that if I _____ you.

   a am   b would be   c were

3 If I _____ more about it, I'd help you.

   a would know   b knew   c know

4 We're going to launch our own _____ .

   a computer   b Internet   c website

5 David would like that joke if he _____ here.

   a were   b would be   c is

6 If you _____ any movie, which one would it be?

   a can watch   b could watch   c watched

7 What _____ they do if we went to the police?

   a would   b will   c were

8 My friend sometimes spends hours _____ the Internet.

   a looking   b surfing   c watching

9 If Mary found that book, she _____ it.

   a 'd buy   b bought   c 'll buy

8

3 Vocabulary

Match the two parts of each word or phrase. Then complete the sentences.

memory	engine	1 I normally use a mouse. I don't like using the _touch pad_ .
search	~~pad~~	2 How many _____ _____ does your new laptop have?
~~touch~~	cord	3 I think Google is the most frequently used _____ _____ .
pro	vider	4 Can you put those files on a _____ _____ for me?
power	ter	5 I can't turn the laptop on. The _____ _____ seems to be broken.
USB	ser	6 Are you happy with your Internet _____ ? Mine doesn't offer a very good service.
brow	board	7 I need an _____ so I can plug my laptop in here.
key	ports	8 Peter has a problem with his _____ . The "R" key doesn't work.
adap	stick	9 I'm using a new Internet _____ , and it's much faster than my old one was.

8

How did you do?

Total: **25**

| Very good 25 – 20 | OK 19 – 16 | Review Unit 14 again 15 or less |

15 Lost worlds

1 Grammar

* Past perfect

a Read the story, and then number the pictures to show the order in which the events happened. Write numbers 1–8 in the boxes.

When Mrs. Johnson got home last Wednesday, she found a terrible mess in her living room. She was afraid, so she immediately called the police and asked them to come to her house. When the police arrived, they found something very strange: The man who had broken into the house was asleep in one of the bedrooms!

The thief had gone into Mrs. Johnson's house and had started to put some things into a big bag. But then he had found some food in the kitchen, and, because he was hungry, he had eaten it all. Feeling sleepy, he had gone into a bedroom, and he had fallen asleep!

b Match the sentences. Write a–h in the boxes.

1 I didn't watch the movie on TV last night. [c]

2 I didn't recognize my cousin.

3 There weren't any books left in the store.

4 I woke up very late yesterday.

5 My mom couldn't use the car.

6 I was happy when I beat Sarah at tennis.

7 My sister had to go to the hospital last week.

8 We really enjoyed our trip to New York City.

a I hadn't turned my alarm clock on the night before.

b We hadn't been there before.

c I'd seen it three times before.

d They'd sold them all.

e She'd hurt herself in a volleyball game.

f He'd changed a lot since the last time I saw him.

g I'd never won a game against her before.

h Our dad had taken her keys with him.

c Complete the sentences with the past perfect form of the verbs in parentheses.

1 When I turned on the TV, the show _had finished_ (finish).

2 I couldn't pay because I _____ (leave) my money at home.

3 I didn't do very well on the test because I _____ (not study) the night before.

4 I went to France last year. It was the first time I _____ (visit) another country.

5 There wasn't any ice cream left because my brother and sister _____ (eat) it all.

6 The store wouldn't exchange the shirt I'd bought because I _____ (lose) the receipt.

7 We couldn't buy a new memory stick because the stores _____ (close).

8 You looked bored at the movies. _____ you _____ (see) the movie before?

d Complete the sentences with the simple past or past perfect form of the verbs in parentheses.

1 When James _arrived_ (arrive) at the station, the train _had left_ (leave).

2 Our neighbor _____ (be) really angry with us because our ball _____ (break) his window.

3 Because I _____ (spend) all my money on CDs, I _____ (not buy) the shirt I wanted.

4 Kylie _____ (not be) pleased when Alex came to her party because she _____ (not invite) him.

5 I lost all my work because I _____ (forget) to save it before the power _____ (go) out!

6 I _____ (look) everywhere for my books, but I couldn't remember where I _____ (put) them.

e Complete the text with the simple past or past perfect form of the verbs in parentheses.

In 1962, Nelson Mandela, the leader of the African National Congress (ANC), was sent to prison for life. The ANC _fought_ (fight) against the idea of apartheid, a system in South Africa that ¹ _____ (not give) black people the same rights as white people. While Mandela ² _____ (be) in prison, he ³ _____ (become) very famous all over the world.

When the South African Government ⁴ _____ (allow) Mandela to leave prison in 1990, he ⁵ _____ (be) a prisoner for more than 27 years. After leaving prison, he ⁶ _____ (continue) to work for all of the people in his country. Mandela and President de Klerk, ⁷ _____ (win) the Nobel Peace Prize in 1993 because they ⁸ _____ (work) very hard for peace.

In 1994, Mandela ⁹ _____ (become) president of South Africa. There ¹⁰ _____ (not be) a black president before him.

2 Pronunciation

*had

a Underline the word *had* where it is stressed. (Circle) the word *had* where it is weak.

1 I <u>had</u> a pizza last night.

2 It was the best pizza I had ever eaten.

3 My mom had a great idea.

4 It was the best idea my mom had ever had.

5 We had a vacation in Alaska last year.

6 My family had always wanted to go there.

b ▶ **CD3 T49** Listen, check and repeat.

3 Vocabulary

★ Noun suffixes: -r, -er, -or and -ist

a Look at pictures 1–10 and fill in the crossword.

Across: 1 JUGGLER

Down: 2 EXPLORER

b Complete the sentences with the correct form of the words in parentheses.

1 My brother's a really good _photographer_ . (photograph)

2 When I was young, I always wanted to be a famous _____ . (explore)

3 My sister always wanted to be a taxi _____ . (drive)

4 I'm sorry, I don't know this town. I'm just a _____ here. (tour)

5 I read in the paper that an _____ has found a new planet. (astronomy)

6 My mother works for a company in the city. She's the _____ . (manage)

7 I'm sure it's interesting to be a _____ and work for a newspaper. (journal)

8 My cousin works for the ABC Company. He's a _____ , but he hopes to be the manager one day! (reception)

9 My dad doesn't like doing things in the house, so we're getting a _____ to do my bedroom. (decorate)

10 I love old things, so when I finish school, I want to be an _____ . (archaeology)

Across

Down

Culture in mind

Complete the sentences with *El Dorado*, *Atlantis* or *Shambhala*. Then check with the text on page 104 of the Student's Book.

1 One story says that the gods decided to destroy _____*Atlantis*_____ because its people had become greedy and wanted more power.

2 Spanish explorers first heard of the legend of _____ in 1537.

3 _____ is the name of a mystical kingdom behind the Himalayas.

4 The Spanish sent a lot of people to look for _____ , but they never found it.

5 Some people say that _____ never existed but was invented by the Greek philosopher Plato.

6 _____ was the name of a chief who covered himself in gold.

5 Study help

★ Vocabulary: suffixes

a Suffixes are added to words to change the part of speech. Study the examples:

- Many suffixes, for example, *-ful*, *-less*, *-able*, change a noun or verb into an adjective. For example, *use*: *useful/useless/usable*.

- Other suffixes, for example, *-er*, *-ist*, *-ation*, change a verb into a noun. For example, *paint*: *painter*; *transform*: *transformation*.

b Underline the suffixes in these words. What part of speech is each one? Write *noun* or *adjective*.

1 art<u>ist</u>   _____*noun*_____   5 comfortable   _____

2 hopeful   _____   6 hopeless   _____

3 programmer _____   7 lovable   _____

4 relaxation   _____   8 imagination   _____

c Add a suffix to each word in the box and write it in the correct column.

archaeology art climb decorate ~~explain~~ inform paint
communicate ~~science~~ swim tour combine violin ~~act~~

-ation	-ist	-er / -or
explanation	*scientist*	*actor*

Skills in mind

6 Listen

▶ **CD3 T50** Greg went to Machu Picchu, in Peru, last year with his father. He is talking to a friend about the trip. Listen and answer the questions. Check (✓) the correct pictures.

1 What time did they take the train from Cuzco?

2 What was it like inside the train?

3 What had happened to the train tracks?

4 What did Greg do after the train accident?

WRITING TIP

How to write a good narrative

Organization

- At the beginning, give the background and include other important information. For example, where did the story happen? Who are the main characters?

- Start a new paragraph for each stage of the story. For example, *1 – the background to the story*; *2 – the main events*; and *3 – the ending*. Make sure your ending is interesting!

Language

- To make your story clear, you need to use the right verb forms: such as simple past, past continuous, or past perfect. Be careful to choose the right one! Remember to use adjectives and adverbs to make the story more interesting.

- Always check your work when you have finished writing! On a test, allow at least five minutes to do this.

---

7 Write

Write a short story about a journey where something went wrong.

Unit check

1 Fill in the blanks

Complete the text by adding the suffixes -r, -er, -ist or -or to the words in parentheses.

I'd like to be a famous soccer _____player_____ (play) like Cristiano Ronaldo, but my father thinks that I should be a ¹_____ (journal) with the local newspaper! My mother thinks it would be better if I became a hotel ²_____ (manage) because that's what she wanted to be! But if I worked in a hotel, I'd want to be the ³_____ (own), of course! I don't want to have a job like my uncle, who's a ⁴_____ (decorate), or my cousin, who's a ⁵_____ (teach) in Miami. Maybe I could be a ⁶_____ (travel) and go around the world with a famous ⁷_____ (explore). Or I could be an amazing ⁸_____ (art) like Picasso. But what I really want to be is a ⁹_____ (cycle) and win the Tour de France!

[ ] 9

2 Choose the correct answers

(Circle) the correct answer: a, b or c.

1 I wanted to see you, but you _____ to Chicago.

   a have gone   b (had gone)   c has gone

2 I _____ Jena for years until I saw her this morning.

   a haven't seen   b did not see   c hadn't seen

3 The movie _____ at four and finished at six.

   a had start   b have started   c started

4 Dad was very happy when he saw that we _____ his car.

   a had washed   b have washed   c washed

5 There _____ any tickets left.

   a hadn't been   b weren't   c wasn't

6 I was really angry when I found out that they _____ you my secret.

   a was telling   b tell   c had told

7 My dad couldn't drive to work yesterday because he _____ the car keys!

   a has lost   b had lost   c was losing

8 I didn't see Taylor because she had left before I _____ .

   a 've arrived   b 'd arrived   c arrived

9 I couldn't give the teacher my homework because I _____ it at home.

   a was leaving   b have left   c had left

[ ] 8

3 Vocabulary

Choose the correct suffix for the words in each group. Then write the word and the part of speech – noun or adjective.

-less	~~-able~~	-er	-ation	-ist

1 comfort   _comfortable_   _adjective_
2 climb   _____   _____
3 hope   _____   _____
4 violin   _____   _____
5 invite   _____   _____

-ful	-ation	-or	-er

6 teach   _____   _____
7 act   _____   _____
8 care   _____   _____
9 inform   _____   _____

[ ] 8

How did you do?

Total: [ ] 25

😊 Very good 25 – 20	😐 OK 19 – 16	🙁 Review Unit 15 again 15 or less

16 A stroke of luck

1 Remember and check

a Complete the summary of the story using words in the box. Then check with the text on page 106 of the Student's Book.

| actor | dancer | dangerous | injury | jumped | lucky | risk |
| storm | ~~success~~ | swim |

The stories about Charlize Theron and Richard Branson show that
¹ _success_ requires more than just luck. Charlize Theron is now a successful ² _____ , but her life has not always been easy. For years, she tried to be a ³ _____ but had to give up that idea because of a knee ⁴ _____ . She had a ⁵ _____ break when she met the talent agent John Crosby in a bank. Then she did her part by taking his advice and working hard to become a better actor.

Businessman Richard Branson has needed more than luck to survive several ⁶ _____ situations. Once he and wife were caught in a bad ⁷ _____ while fishing in the ocean near Mexico. Branson saw that if they didn't try to ⁸ _____ to shore, they would die. So he and his wife ⁹ _____ into the water and swam two miles to the shore. This ¹⁰ _____ saved their lives. Theron and Branson have been lucky, but they have also worked hard and taken risks when necessary.

b Match the two parts of the sentences. Then check with the text on page 106 of the Student's Book.

1 If Theron hadn't injured her knee,
2 If Theron hadn't had an argument at the bank,
3 Theron wouldn't have become an actor
4 Branson and his wife would have died
5 If Theron and Branson had given up,
6 If Branson's friends had swum to shore,

a they might not have died.
b if they hadn't swum to shore.
c she would have become a dancer.
d they wouldn't have been successful.
e she wouldn't have met Crosby.
f if she hadn't taken Crosby's advice.

2 Grammar

✱ Reported statements

a Complete the table. Write the grammar descriptions and the example sentences.

DIRECT SPEECH	REPORTED SPEECH
Simple present	**Simple past**
I'm a writer.	She said she was a writer.
Present _continuous_	**Past** _continuous_
I'm writing a book about luck.	She said she _was writing_ a book about luck.
Present _____	_____
They've never been to Dallas.	They said they _____ to Dallas.
Simple past	_____
We arrived last week.	They said they _____ the week before.
am/ is/ are going to	_____ **going to**
My uncle's going to live in Lima.	He said his uncle _____ in Lima.
can/can't	_____ / _____
I can't come on Saturday.	She said she _____ on Saturday.
will/ won't	_____ / _____
I'll go next week.	He said he _____ the following week.

b Read the dialogue. Then complete the paragraph using reported speech.

Woman: Excuse me. I need some help.

Me: Oh, OK. I'll be happy to help you.

Woman: I've never been here before, and someone stole my purse this morning.

Me: Well, I'm sorry. I don't have any money.

Woman: No, that's OK. I don't want money. I'm trying to find the police station.

Me: Oh, I see. Well, I'm going that way, so I can take you there.

Woman: Great! Thank you very much.

Yesterday a woman came up to me in town. She looked worried and said she _needed_ some help. I felt sorry for her, so I said I [1]_____ happy to help her. She told me she [2]_____ to this town before, and she said that someone [3]_____ her purse that morning. I said I [4]_____ sorry but I [5]_____ any money. The woman said that she [6]_____ money and that she [7]_____ to find the police station. So I told her that I [8]_____ that way, and that I [9]_____ her there. She was very happy!

c ▶ CD3 T51 Sophia, Claudia, Josh and Mitsuko are talking about an amusement park. Listen to what they said about the park. Who likes it? Who doesn't like it?

d ▶ CD3 T51 Listen again. Complete the summaries. Use reported speech.

Sophia and Claudia, from Italy

Josh, from the United States

Sophia and Claudia said they _had arrived_ there at [1]_____ . They said that some of the rides [2]_____ , but they also said the lines [3]_____ and they [4]_____ it [5]_____ very expensive there.

Josh told me he thought it [6]_____ place. He said all the rides [7]_____ , but his [8]_____ *The Elevator*. He said [9]_____ three times and that he [10]_____ again.

Mitsuko, from Japan

Mitsuko said that she [11]_____ the park very much. She said that [12]_____ very scary, and she said she [13]_____ them. She also told me that she [14]_____ there again.

3 Vocabulary

✱ Noun suffixes, with *-ation* and *-ment*

a Find and (circle) the noun forms of the verbs in the box.

~~calculate~~	cancel	explain	equip	act
improve	inform	manage	agree	

C	E	E	I	M	P	R	O	V	E	M	E	N	T
A	D	Q	N	A	E	Q	I	I	N	P	M	T	Z
L	U	U	F	N	X	S	N	J	T	E	R	I	E
C	C	I	O	G	P	A	A	Q	E	X	P	M	N
U	A	P	R	A	L	L	G	U	Q	P	F	A	T
L	U	M	M	G	A	G	R	E	U	L	E	N	T
A	F	E	A	T	N	V	O	S	P	A	G	A	R
T	G	N	T	I	A	C	T	I	O	N	A	G	E
I	N	T	I	O	N	O	I	O	N	A	R	E	D
O	B	C	O	M	M	E	N	A	M	T	E	M	N
N	O	R	N	K	P	O	S	E	E	I	E	E	D
C	A	N	C	E	L	L	A	T	I	O	N	N	E
S	I	N	A	G	R	E	E	M	E	N	T	T	O

b Rewrite the sentences, using the nouns from the grid in Exercise 3a.

1 My brother explained the math problem. His _explanation_ helped me understand it.

2 We sold our house after we had improved it a lot. It sold because we had made a lot of _____s to it.

3 The people here don't manage things very well. The _____ here isn't very good.

4 They informed us about a lot of things. They gave us a lot of _____ .

5 We calculated how much money we needed to spend. We made a _____ to see how much money we needed to spend.

6 They've canceled the meeting. Please tell everyone about the _____ .

7 We're going to the mountains for a few days, so we'll need some camping _____ .

4 🔲 Vocabulary bank

Complete the sentences with the words in the box.

potluck	superstitious	all the luck
knock on wood	by chance	
fingers crossed	~~good luck~~	bad luck

1 Some people say that a horseshoe can bring you _good luck_ .

2 We didn't know which restaurant was best, so we just took _____ and ate at the first one we came to.

3 I have my math test tomorrow. Please keep your _____ _____ for me.

4 A: I found a lottery ticket on the ground, and I won!

   B: Really? Well, some people have _____ !

5 I hadn't heard of the movie before. I saw it _____ on TV. It was fantastic!

6 A: Tomorrow is Friday the 13th, and it's my birthday. That'll bring me _____ !

   B: Don't be _____ ! It might bring you good luck!

7 Peter's promised to be here at 8:30 tomorrow, so we'll start at nine o'clock, _____ .

5 Grammar

✱ Third conditional

For each pair of sentences, write one sentence in the third conditional.

1 Alex was late for school. The teacher was angry with him.

If Alex hadn't been late for school, the
teacher wouldn't have been angry with him.

2 Alex didn't listen to the questions. He got all the answers wrong.

If Alex had listened _____

_____ .

3 He got all the answers wrong. The other kids laughed at him.

If he hadn't _____

_____ .

4 The other kids laughed at him. He felt really miserable.

He wouldn't _____

_____ .

5 He felt really miserable. He ate a huge lunch.

_____

_____

_____ .

6 He ate a huge lunch. He had a stomachache.

_____

_____

_____ .

6 Pronunciation

✱ *would have ('ve) / wouldn't have*

a ▶ **CD3 T52** Listen and repeat.

1 I would've gone.
2 She would've told you.
3 They wouldn't have done it.
4 We would've eaten before.

b ▶ **CD3 T53** Listen and repeat.

1 I would've gone to the party if I hadn't been sick.
2 She would've told you if she'd known.
3 They wouldn't have done it if you'd been there.
4 We would've eaten before if we'd been hungry.

7 Everyday English

Complete the dialogues. Use the expressions in the box.

> it's a little like   If only I'd
> what's going on   was like
> ~~have a word~~   it's just that

A **Sally:** Louise? Can I ¹ *have a word* with you?

Louise: Of course, Sally. Why? Is something wrong?

Sally: No, not really.
² _____ I want to talk to someone about Patrick.

Louise: You mean, your boyfriend Patrick? OK, so tell me,
³ _____ ?

B **Jamie:** I had an argument with my dad last night. I broke a plate and he
⁴ _____ "Why can't you be more careful?," you know?

Oliver: Yeah, I know!
⁵ _____ when I lost my mom's camera. She really yelled at me. She said, " ⁶ _____ said no when you asked to borrow it! Then this wouldn't have happened."

Skills in mind

8 Study help

✳ How to review

Read these tips to help you to review for your exams:

- Look again at your scores in the *Check your progress* sections of the Student's Book. Which areas of grammar or vocabulary did you do well in? Which areas did you do less well in?

- For the things that you didn't do well in, read the examples, rules and exercises in the Student's Book again carefully. Do the same with the *Unit checks* in this Workbook.

- Check through your Workbook. Are there any exercises that you haven't done yet? Do them now!

- It is also a good idea to repeat some exercises that you did well in before.

9 Read

a Read this letter to the newspaper. Did the writer enjoy the movie?

b Write T (true), F (false) or N (not in the text).

1 Philip Lawrence wrote a review of the movie *Slumdog Millionaire*. | T |

2 James disagrees with everything Philip Lawrence said. | |

3 James saw the movie last week. | |

4 James thought that the acting was good but the directing wasn't. | |

5 James thinks that the movie director didn't choose the right actor. | |

6 Lawrence thinks that American movies are better than movies made in foreign countries. | |

7 James didn't like the last Hollywood movie he saw. | |

8 James thinks that movie tickets are too expensive. | |

<u>Dear</u> Sir or Madam:

Last week I read Philip Lawrence's review of the movie *Slumdog Millionaire* and I am writing to say that, in my view, Mr. Lawrence was wrong about everything he said.

¹ _____ , he said that the movie was not good enough to be nominated for the Oscars, ² _____ I thought the movie was an excellent production, with very high quality acting and directing. I enjoyed it very much.

³ _____ , Mr. Lawrence said that the young actor Dev Patel was not a good choice ⁴ _____ he "was not an experienced actor." Personally, ⁵ _____ that Patel gave an excellent performance, even though he hasn't had much acting experience. The movie would not have been better if the director had chosen a trained teenage actor.

⁶ _____ , Mr. Lawrence said that the story and the characters were not believable, that nothing like this could happen. But ⁷ _____ I think that the movie gives a realistic picture of the problems people have in many places in the world today.

Sincerely,

James Singleton

WRITING TIP

Review

In other units in this Workbook, you have seen ideas to help you with your writing. These include:

- making your writing more interesting (Unit 4)

- using linking words like *first of all, secondly* etc. (Unit 5)

- writing informal letters and emails (Unit 7)

- using linking words like *then, finally* etc. (Unit 11)

- how to write a good narrative (Unit 15)

Complete the letter in Exercise 9a with the words in the box.

but   second   I think   first of all
in my opinion   ~~dear~~   because   finally

Unit check

1 Fill in the blanks

Complete the text with nouns made from the verbs in the box.

> educate   equip   improve   calculate   manage   entertain   communicate   ~~inform~~

Yesterday, the people at Millers & Co. got some _information_ from the company's ¹_____ . They said the new office ²_____ should not be used for watching DVDs or any other kind of ³_____ . They said that the recent ⁴_____s to the computer system were intended to provide better ⁵_____ between the company and the customers. The manager had done some ⁶_____ s, and they show that watching DVDs during office hours may cost the company over $35,000 per year. Millers & Co. plans to introduce training courses which will lead to better ⁷_____ for the employees. **7**

2 Choose the correct answers

(Circle) the correct answer: a, b or c.

1   Mom told me that she _____ me to help.
   a (wanted)   b wanting   c want

2   I asked them where they _____ for their next vacation.
   a were going   b had gone   c go

3   Alyssa told me she _____ drive me to school.
   a could   b has   c could be

4   She asked me if we _____ hungry.
   a have   b was   c were

5   We asked her what she _____ us to do.
   a has wanted   b want   c wanted

6   I asked Tom why he _____ his promise.
   a had forgotten   b forget   c forgets

7   He asked her if she _____ to Austin.
   a had been   b was   c been

8   They would have invited you if _____ you.
   a they saw   b they've seen   c they'd seen

9   If I'd known the answer, I _____ you.
   a would have told   b had told   c would tell

10   If Kate _____ a lot of homework, we could have gone out together.
   a hadn't had   b hadn't   c wouldn't have

9

3 Vocabulary

Complete the sentences with nouns made from the verbs in the box.

> ~~improve~~   treat   react   accommodate   pay
> cancel   invite   reserve   calculate   inform

1   The new DVD player wasn't an _improvement_ . The old one was better.

2   That restaurant is always full. I think we should make a _____ .

3   Sorry, but we only accept _____ by credit card.

4   I'm not going to her party. I didn't get an _____ .

5   You lost her DVD? What was her _____ when you told her?

6   I didn't like staying in that tent. Next time, I want better _____ !

7   The hotel's full. We'll only get a room if there's a _____ .

8   Can you give us some _____ about the city?

9   Scientists have discovered a new _____ for this illness.

10   I've done a quick _____ , and it's clear we need more money!

9

How did you do?

Total: **25**

| Very good 25 – 20 | OK 19 – 16 |  Review Unit 16 again 15 or less |

Vocabulary bank

Unit 3 phrases with *get*

1 to get home = to arrive at your home
   I usually **get home** from school at about five o'clock.

2 to get together = to meet with other people
   My friends and I **get together** on Sundays to play soccer in the park.

3 to get a [phone] call
   I **got** five **calls** last night while I was working.

4 to get sick
   When we were on vacation, my sister **got sick** because she drank water from the faucet.

5 to get somewhere/anywhere = to improve, to make progress
   I started learning Spanish last year, but I'm not **getting anywhere** so I think I'll stop.

6 to get hot/cold/warm
   It's **getting** really **cold** now. Let's go back into the house.

7 to get hungry/thirsty
   I'm **getting hungry**. Can we have lunch soon?

8 to get going = to start (something) / to leave
   Look! It's almost ten o'clock. I think we should **get going**, or we'll be late.

9 to get a/the chance
   I'm really busy now, but I'll call you if I **get a chance**.

10 to get pleasure (from)
    I'm not very good at table tennis, but I **get** a lot of **pleasure** from playing it.

Unit 4 sports

1 a stadium
   The **stadium** holds 60,000 people.

2 a championship
   He won the **championship** for the fifth time.

3 to score
   He **scored** a great goal.

4 a goal/point
   In soccer, you score **goals**, and in basketball you score **points**.

5 to tie / a tie
   The game was **tied**, 3–3. It was a tie.

6 a reserve
   I didn't play.
   I was a **reserve**.

7 to substitute
   He was **substituted** after 30 minutes.

8 a record
   It's a new world **record**!

9 to hold a/the record
   He **holds the record** for the marathon.

10 to break a record
    She **broke** the world record for the 100-meter race.

Unit 6 North American and British English

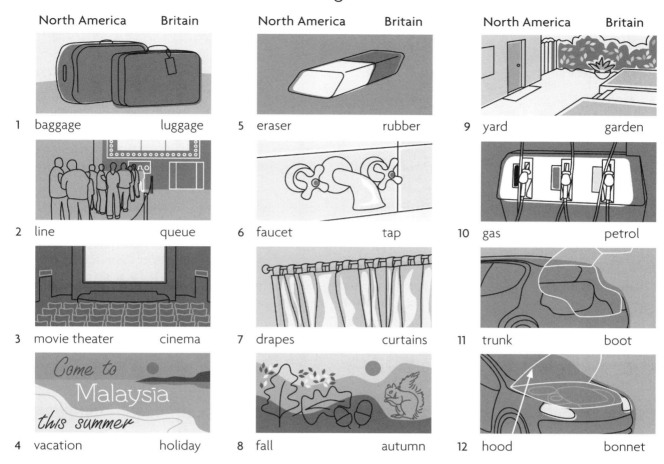

North America	Britain		North America	Britain		North America	Britain
1 baggage	luggage		5 eraser	rubber		9 yard	garden
2 line	queue		6 faucet	tap		10 gas	petrol
3 movie theater	cinema		7 drapes	curtains		11 trunk	boot
4 vacation	holiday		8 fall	autumn		12 hood	bonnet

Unit 7 talking about age

1 adulthood = the time of life when you are an adult
Adulthood brings responsibility.

2 childhood = the time of life when you are a child
She didn't have a very happy **childhood**.

3 adolescence = the time of life when you are a teenager/adolescent
Some people think **adolescence** is the best time of your life!

4 youth = the time of life when you are young
My grandmother says the world was very different **in her youth**.

5 to get/grow old(er)
My dad always says he isn't worried about **getting older**.

6 to be getting on = to get/grow old
He was a good athlete when he was 25, but he's **getting on** in years now.

7 underage = too young to do something (because of a law)
You have to be 16 to watch that movie. I'm only 15, so I'm **underage**.

8 to come of age = to reach the age when you are legally an adult
In most states in the U.S., people **come of age** when they are 18.

9 to look [your] age = to look the age that you really are
He looks like he's 20, but really he's 40! He doesn't **look his age** at all.

10 to act [your] age = <u>not</u> to behave as if you were a child (or younger than you really are)
Oh, Jimmy! You're not six years old any more! You're 15! **Act your age!**

Unit 8 – verb and noun pairs

have

1 an accident
   James is in the hospital. He **had an accident** in his car.

2 a problem
   I **have a problem**. I want to buy that shirt, but I don't have any money.

3 an idea
   We didn't know what to do, but then Alice **had an idea**.

4 a meal
   Last night we all went out to a restaurant and **had a** really nice **meal** together.

make

5 a suggestion = to suggest
   Can I **make a suggestion**? Why don't we go to the movies tonight?

6 an offer = to offer
   I didn't want to sell my bike, but somebody **made** me **an offer** of $100, so I sold it.

7 a decision = to decide
   I don't know which one to buy, but I need to **make a decision** quickly.

8 progress = to get better
   My German is getting better and better. I'm **making** a lot of **progress**.

take

9 a test / an exam = to take a test
   My mother **took** her driving **test** last week and she passed!

10 [your] time = not to do something quickly
   We aren't late, so we can **take** our **time** and not hurry.

11 a break = to stop work for a short time
   We worked for three hours, and then we **took a break** and had some coffee.

12 an interest [in] = show interest
   We really like our teacher because she **takes an interest** in all of us.

Unit 9 – disasters

1   to be on fire

It was terrible. When they went home, they saw that their house **was on fire**.

2   to set fire to

We think someone **set fire to** our car.

3   to catch (on) fire

It was so hot and dry that trees in the forest **caught on fire**.

4   to put a fire out

A fire engine came, and the firefighters **put the fire out**.

5   to crack

A stone hit the window and **cracked** the glass.

6   to collapse

The earthquake was so strong that many buildings **collapsed**.

7   to be starving

The floods destroyed crops, and many people **were starving**.

8   to be homeless

Thousands of people **were homeless** after the earthquake destroyed their houses.

Unit 10 – houses/homes

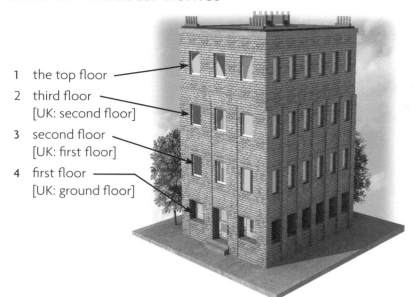

1 the top floor
2 third floor
   [UK: second floor]
3 second floor
   [UK: first floor]
4 first floor
   [UK: ground floor]

11 to move

12 to share a room

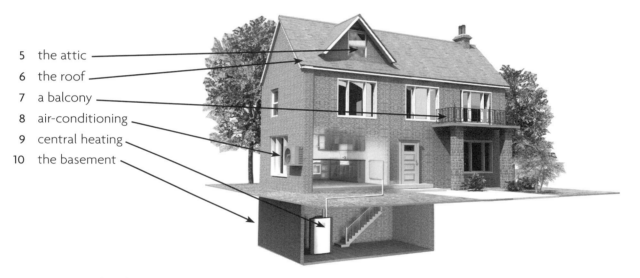

5 the attic
6 the roof
7 a balcony
8 air-conditioning
9 central heating
10 the basement

Unit 11 – thinking

1	knowledge	Her **knowledge** of African countries is amazing.
2	a belief	It's my **belief** that violence on TV is a bad thing.
3	a thought	It's an interesting idea. Do you have any **thoughts** about it?
4	concentration	Someone knocked on the door and broke my **concentration**.
5	imagination	You need a lot of **imagination** to write good stories.
6	inspiration	A beautiful sunset was my **inspiration** for this poem.
7	an estimate	I think it's going to cost about $200, but that's just my **estimate**.
8	a guess	Sorry, you're wrong, but it was a good **guess** anyway!

Unit 12 – music and musical instruments

1 an orchestra

2 the conductor

3 a choir

4 lyrics

5 percussion

6 backup singers

7 a recording studio

8 to be on tour

9 an open-air concert

Unit 13 – medicine

1 an operation

2 medicine

3 a bandage

4 [to be in / to have (a foot) in] a cast

5 [to be on] crutches

6 [to be in] a wheelchair

7 to take [someone's] temperature

8 to take [someone's] blood pressure

9 a prescription = a piece of paper a doctor gives you in order to get medicine
I took the **prescription** to the pharmacist and got the pills.

10 allergic [to something] = unable to eat something because it makes you sick
I'm **allergic to** cheese. If I eat cheese, I get a stomachache.

11 to come down with something = to get an illness or disease
I was feeling fine, but then suddenly I **came down with** a really bad cold.

12 to get over [an illness] = to recover and get better
My dad got a very bad cold. He's OK now, but it took him a week to **get over** it.

Unit 14 – electrical matters

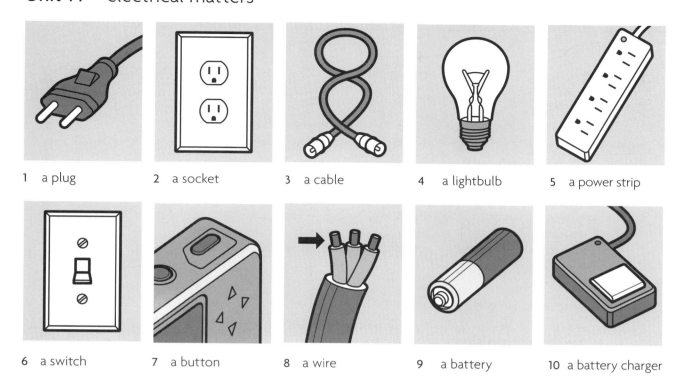

1   a plug   2   a socket   3   a cable   4   a lightbulb   5   a power strip

6   a switch   7   a button   8   a wire   9   a battery   10 a battery charger

Unit 16 – luck

1   Good luck!

    A: I have a very important exam tomorrow.

    B: Really? Well, **good luck**! I hope you do well.

2   Bad luck!

    A: It was very close. I almost won, but in the end, I came in second.

    B: Oh, what **bad luck**! Still, second's very good, isn't it?

3   [to take] potluck = to just choose anything, without knowing which is best

    A: We didn't know which movie to go to, so we just picked one and went in.

    B: Oh, kind of **potluck**, you mean?

4   [to keep your] fingers crossed = to hope that someone has good luck

    A: I have a job interview tomorrow. I really want to get the job!

    B: Well, I'll **keep my fingers crossed** for you.

5   [to] knock on wood = if [I'm/we're] lucky

    A: You're going on a picnic tomorrow, aren't you?

    B: Yes. They say the weather's going to be sunny, **knock on wood**!

6   Some people have all the luck!

    A: My dad's taking me to his office tomorrow, so I'm going to miss the test.

    B: Really? Wow! **Some people have all the luck**! I wish I could miss the test, too.

7   by chance = not in a planned way

    A: So, you saw Annie yesterday?

    B: Yes I did. I ran into her in town **by chance**.

8   superstitious = believing that some things bring good or bad luck

    A: Oh, no! I broke the mirror! That's going to bring me seven years of bad luck!

    B: Oh, don't **be superstitious**. It's just a mirror!

Grammar reference

Unit 3

Past continuous

1 We use the past continuous to talk about actions in progress at a certain time in the past.
*In 1999, we **were living** in California.   The television was on, but I **wasn't watching** it.*

2 The past continuous is formed with the simple past of *be* + verb + *-ing*.
*You **were running** very fast.*   *You **weren't running** very fast.*
*Andy **was listening** to the radio.*   *Andy **wasn't watching** television.*

3 The question is formed with the simple past of *be* + subject + verb + *-ing*.
Was James running?   *Yes, he **was**. / No, he **wasn't**.*
*Were your parents **having** lunch?*   *Yes, they **were**. / No, they **weren't**.*
*What **were** you **studying**?*
*Why **was** she **crying**?*

Past continuous vs. simple past

1 When we talk about the past, we use the simple past for actions that happened at one particular time. We use the past continuous for background actions.
*When my friend **arrived**, I **was having** lunch.   He **was driving** too fast, and he **had** an accident.*
*What **did** you **say**? I **wasn't listening**.*

2 We often use *when* with the simple past and *while* with the past continuous.
*I was sleeping **when** the phone rang.   **While** Jack was washing the dishes, he dropped a plate.*

Unit 4

Comparative and superlative adjectives

1 When we want to compare two things, or two groups of things, we use a comparative form + *than*.
*I'm **taller than** my father.   DVDs are **more expensive than** CDs.   His watch is **better than** mine.*

2 With short adjectives, we normally add *-er*: *cold – colder   long – longer   smart – smarter*

If the adjective ends in *e*, we add only *-r*: *white – whiter   safe – safer*

If the adjective ends with consonant + *-y*, we change the *y* to *i* and add *-er*.
easy – easier   early – earlier   happy – happier

If the adjective ends in one vowel + one consonant, we double the final consonant and add *-er*.
big – bigger   fat – fatter   thin – thinner

3 With longer adjectives (two or more syllables), we use *more* + the adjective.
*expensive – **more** expensive   boring – **more** boring*

4 Some adjectives have a different comparative form.
*good – **better**   bad – **worse**   far – **farther***

5 We can modify the comparison by using *much*, *a lot* or *a little*. These words come before the normal comparison.
*This movie is **much** better than the book.   His pronunciation is **a lot** worse than mine.*
*We walked **a little** farther today than last week.*

Adverbs

1 We use adverbs to describe verbs. Adverbs say how an action is or was performed.
*She <u>smiled</u> **happily**.   <u>Drive</u> **slowly**!   We <u>got</u> to school **late**.*

We can also use adverbs before adjectives.
*It was **bitterly** <u>cold</u> yesterday.   The water was **incredibly** <u>warm</u>, so we went swimming.*

2   Most adverbs are formed by adjective + -ly: *quiet – quietly*   *bad – badly*

If the adjective ends in *-le*, we drop the *-e* and add *-y*: *terrible – terribly*   *comfortable – comfortably*

If the adjective ends in consonant + -y, we change the *y* to *i* and add *-ly*.
easy – easily   *happy – happily*   *lucky – luckily*

3   Some adverbs are irregular. They don't have an *-ly* ending.
*good – **well**   fast – **fast**   hard – **hard**   early – **early**   late – **late***

Comparative adverbs

1   To compare adverbs, we use the same rules as we do when we compare adjectives. With short adverbs that don't end in -ly, we add -er or -r, and *than* after the adverb.
*I was late for school, but my brother was **later than** me!*

2   With longer adverbs, we use *more* + adverb + *than*.
*I ran **more quickly than** the others.*

3   To compare the adverb *well*, we use *better … than*. To compare the adverb *far*, we use *farther … than*.
*Steve plays tennis **better than** I do.*   *My school is **farther** from my house **than** the park.*

Unit 5

will/won't, or *might (not) / may (not)* for prediction

1   We can use the modal verb *will ('ll)* or *will not (won't)* to make predictions about the future.
*Don't worry about the exam next week. It **won't be** difficult.*

2   We use *might/might not* or *may/may not* to make less certain predictions about the future.
*I'm not sure, but I think I **might go** to college when I finish high school.*

3   Like all modal verbs, *will/won't* and *might/might not* and *may/may not* are followed by the base form of the main verb, and the form is the same for all subjects.
*I think it'll **be** a nice day tomorrow.* (**NOT** ~~I think it'll to be a nice day tomorrow.~~)
My brother might go to live in Europe. (**NOT** ~~My brother might to go to live in Europe.~~)
She may not pass her driving test.

4   We make questions with *will* by putting the subject **after** the modal verb.
***Will** we **have** a test next week?*

First conditional

1   We often make conditional sentences by using *If* + subject + present simple in the *if* clause and *will/won't / might/ might not* in the main clause.
***If we have** time, **we'll do** some shopping at the supermarket.*
***I might go** out tonight **if there's** nothing good on TV.*

2   We can also use the word *unless* in conditional sentences. It means *if … not*.
***Unless** the teacher explains, we won't know what to do.* (= ***If** the teacher **doesn't** explain, we won't know what to do.*)
*James won't know **unless** you tell him.* (= *James won't know **if** you **don't** tell him.*)

3   There are two clauses in these sentences. We can put the main clause first, or the *if/unless* clause first.
When the *if/unless* clause comes first, there is a comma after it.
Unless the teacher explains, we won't know what to do.
We won't know what to do unless the teacher explains.

Unit 6

Tag questions

1   Tag questions are affirmative or negative questions at the end of statements. We add "tags" to the end of statements:

   a)   when **we are not sure** that what we are saying is correct, and we want the other person to say if we are correct or not.

   b)   when **we are almost sure** that what we are saying is correct, and we want the other person to confirm it.

2   Tags in (a) above have rising intonation: *A: You're French, **aren't you**?*   *B: No, I'm not. I'm Swiss.*

Tags in (b) above have falling intonation: *A: You're French, **aren't you**?*   *B: Yes. I'm from Lyon.*

3   With **affirmative** statements, we use a **negative** tag question: *I'm late, **aren't I**?*   *He's lazy, **isn't he**?*

With **negative** statements, we use an **affirmative** tag question: *I'm not late, **am I**?*   *He isn't lazy, **is he**?*

Present perfect

1   We use the present perfect (present tense of *have* + past participle) to talk about a present situation, and the events in the past that are connected to the present situation.
*The teacher's angry because we **haven't done** our homework.*   *I've **eaten** too much food, and I **feel** sick.*

2   There is an important difference between *have gone* and *have been*.
*My friend Sarah **has been** to Peru on vacation. (= Sarah went to Peru, <u>and she has come back again</u>.)*
*My friend Sarah **has gone** to Peru on vacation. (= Sarah went to Peru, and <u>she is still there</u>.)*

Present perfect + *already/yet/just*

1   We often use the words *already* and *yet* with the present perfect. We use *already* in affirmative sentences and *yet* in negative sentences and in questions.

     The word *already* usually comes between *have* and the past participle. The word *yet* usually comes at the end of the sentence or question.
*I don't want to watch the movie on TV tonight. I**'ve already seen** it.*
*I started this work two hours ago, but I **haven't finished** it **yet**.*

2   When we use the word *just* with the present perfect, it means "not very long ago." Like *already*, *just* is usually placed between *have* and the past participle.
*I**'ve just heard** that my favorite band has released a new CD.*
*Do you want a piece of cake? My mother**'s just made it**.*

Unit 7

Present passive

1   We use the passive when it isn't important to know who does the action, or when we don't know who does it.
*A lot of movies **were made** about the war. (It's not important to know who made them.)*
*That house **was built** in 1852. (I don't know who built it.)*

2   To form the present passive, we use the simple present of the verb *to be* + the past participle of the main verb: *Soccer **is played** in many countries.*   *The animals in the zoo **are fed** every day.*

let/be allowed to

1   We use *be allowed to* to say that you do (or don't) have permission to do something.
*At my school, we **are allowed to** wear jeans.*   *You **aren't allowed to** skateboard in the park.*

2   We use *let* to say that someone gives you, or doesn't give you, permission to do something.
*I **let** my brother borrow my bicycle sometimes.*   *Our teacher **didn't let** us use dictionaries for the test.*

3   Both *let* and *be allowed to* are followed by the infinitive.
*I'm not allowed to **watch** the late-night movie.*   *My dad didn't let me **watch** the late-night movie.*

4   With *let*, the structure is *let* + person + the base form of the verb (without *to*).
*She **didn't let me answer** the question.*   *I'm not going to **let you borrow** my CD player.*

Unit 8

Present perfect with *for* and *since*

1   We can use the present perfect to talk about something that began in the past and continues to be true in the present.
*I **have lived** here for ten years. (= I started living here ten years ago, and I still live here.)*

2   We talk about the time between when something started and now with *for* or *since*.

     We use the word *for* when we mention *a period of time* from the past until now.
*for **an hour**   for **two years**   for **a long time***

     We use the word *since* when we mention a *point in time* in the past.
*since **ten o'clock**   since **1992**   since **last Saturday***

Unit 9

Past passive

1 We form the past passive with the simple past of the verb *to be* and the past participle of the main verb.
*The car **was destroyed** in the accident, and two people **were injured**.*

2 We use the passive when it isn't important to know who does the action, or when we don't know who does it (see Unit 7).

3 Sometimes when we use the passive (present or past), we want to say who or what did the action. To do this, we use the word *by* + noun.
The movie Avatar <u>was directed</u> **by James Cameron.**   *He <u>was arrested</u> **by the police**.*

a(n) and *the*

1 We use *a* or *an* (the indefinite articles) when we are talking about something for the **first** time.
*We've just bought **a** new car.   We watched **a** movie last night.*

We also use *a/an* with a noun when we are talking about something in general, and not a special example of something.
*I think it's nicer to live in **a** house than in **an** apartment.   Let's go and have **a** pizza.*

2 We use *the* (the definite article) with a noun when it is clear which thing or person we are talking about. Sometimes this is when we talk about something for the **second** time.
*I took a photograph of my sister, but **the** photograph was awful!*

Sometimes we use *the* because there is only one of the thing we are talking about.
***The** sun is really hot today. (= There is only one sun.)*

Other times we use it because the person we are talking to already knows which thing we mean.
*Can I use **the** computer now? (= The listener knows which computer you are talking about.)*

3 We also use *the* when we talk about certain things in general, for example, *the movies, the telephone, the Internet.*
*I really like going to **the movies**. (= the movies as a general place, not a particular movie theater)*

Unit 10

too many/much, not enough

1 *too many* and *too much* are phrases that we use to say that there is more of something than is wanted.
*I have **too many CDs**. (= I don't have a place to put all the CDs that I have.)*

2 We use *too many* before plural countable nouns.
*There are **too many cars** on the streets.   I think we have **too many tests**.*

3 We use *too much* before uncountable nouns.
*Don't put **too much water** on the plants.   Don't spend **too much money** in that store.*

4 *Not enough* is the opposite of *too much / too many.* We use this phrase to say that more is needed.
*There aren't **enough** people here to play a volleyball game. (= We need more people.)*

5 *Not enough* is used with plural countable nouns, or with uncountable nouns. We put *not* with the verb, and *enough* before the noun.
*We don't have **enough glasses**, and there isn't **enough soda** for everyone.*

will vs. *be going to*

1 We can use *be going to* or *will* to talk about the future, but there are some differences in meaning.

2 We use *be going to* when we talk about something in the future that is a result of what we can see now, or that we know now.
*Look at those black clouds in the sky! It**'s going to** rain.*

3 We use *be going to* when we talk about our (or other people's) intentions and plans for the future.
*We**'re going to play** volleyball this afternoon. (= We've already decided to do this.)*

4 We often use *will* when we decide to do something at the moment of speaking.
*I'm bored. I think I**'ll go** for a walk.*

Unit 11

Indefinite pronouns: *everyone / no one*, etc.

1   We can use the words *every/some/no* together with *one/thing/where to* make compound nouns.

2   These words mean:

everyone = *all the people*	someone = *a person, but we don't know who*	no one = *none of the people*
everything = *all the things*	something = *a thing, but we don't know which*	nothing = *none of the things*
everywhere = *all the places*	somewhere = *a place, but we don't know where*	nowhere = *none of the places*

3   These words are all singular.

*Something's wrong.   No one's perfect.   Nothing **was** found.   Everywhere **was** full.   Someone **has** taken my pen.*

4   We don't use negative verbs with *nothing* and *no one*.

*I **don't know anyone** here. OR I know no one here.* (NOT ~~I don't know no one here.~~)

5   With other nouns and pronouns, we use *all of/some of/none of* + plural or uncountable noun/pronoun.

***All of** the CDs are mine.   **Some of** the teachers are really nice.   **None of** my friends came to my party.*

must/must not vs. *don't have to*

1   *must not* is the negative of *must*. We use *must not* to say that something is the wrong thing to do, or when we give someone an obligation **not** to do something (American English doesn't usually use the contraction *mustn't*.)

*Teacher: Be quiet! You **must not talk** during the test.*

2   *don't/doesn't have to* is the negative of *have to*. We use *don't/doesn't have to* to say that something is not necessary.

*I love Sundays because I **don't have to get up** early.*

Unit 12

Present perfect continuous

1   The present perfect continuous is formed with the present tense of *have* + *been* + the *-ing* form of the verb.

*I'**ve been waiting** for two hours.   It'**s been raining** since last weekend.*

2   Sentences with the present perfect always connect the present and the past. We often use the present perfect continuous to talk about situations that started in the past and are still continuing now.

*I'**ve been waiting** for two hours. (= I started waiting two hours ago, and I am still waiting.)*

3   We also use the present perfect continuous to talk about actions with a result in the present. These actions may or may not be complete.

*I'**m tired** because I'**ve been working** hard.*

4   We also use the present perfect continuous to talk about actions that began in the past and continue to the present, but perhaps we are not doing the action at the time of speaking.

*I'**ve been studying** English for two years. (= I started studying two years ago, and I am still studying it, but I'm not studying it at this moment.)*

Present perfect and present perfect continuous

1   We use the present perfect to show that an action is finished or to focus on what we have completed in a period of time.

*I'**ve written** a letter.   I'**ve written** three letters this morning.*

2   We use the present perfect continuous to show that an action is still going on or to focus on how long something has been in progress.

*I'**ve been reading** this book for two hours.   I'**ve been reading** detective stories for years.*

3   There are some verbs that cannot usually be used in the continuous. These verbs often express a permanent state. For example, *know, understand, have* (for possession), *like, hate*. For these verbs, we use the present perfect (see also Unit 1 simple present and present continuous).

*She'**s known** her teacher since she was in the first class.* (NOT ~~She's been knowing ...~~)

Unit 13

Defining relative clauses

1   A defining relative clause is something we use to say exactly who or what we are talking about.
*The boy was friendly. The boy **who told me that joke** was friendly.*

2   To make these clauses, we use these words: *who/whose/that/where*. We use *who*, *whose* or *that* for people. The word *whose* shows possession. We use *that* for things and animals. We use *where* for places.
*He's <u>the man</u> **who** told me. OR He's <u>the man</u> **that** told me.*

used to

1   We can use the expression *used to* when we want to talk about an action that happened regularly in the past but doesn't happen anymore.
*My dad **used to** dance. (= My dad danced in the past, but he doesn't dance anymore.)*

2   *used to* is followed by the base form of the main verb.
*Our town **used to be** much smaller than it is now.*

3   The negative of *used to* is *didn't use to*.
*I **didn't use to** eat vegetables. (= In the past I didn't eat vegetables, but now I eat them.)*

We make questions with *used to* using *Did* + subject + *use to* …?
***Did** you **use to live** in Toronto?*

The negative of *used to* and questions with *used to* are not written or said very often.

4   For actions that happened only once in the past, use the simple past.
*I **got married** last year. (**NOT** ~~I used to get married~~ …)*

Unit 14

Second conditional

1   We use the second conditional to talk about unreal or imagined situations in the present or future.
*If I **were a movie star**, I **would live** in a house in Hollywood. (= I am <u>not</u> a movie star, and I <u>don't live</u> in a house in Hollywood.)*
*Your parents **wouldn't take care of** you if they didn't love you. (= Your parents <u>do</u> take care of you because they <u>do</u> love you.)*

2   Sentences in the second conditional have two parts or "clauses": an *If* clause and a main clause.

If clause	Main clause
If + simple past	*would/wouldn't* + main verb
If my brother **had** more time,	*he'd help* me with my homework.
If Jenny **were** older,	*she'd leave* school and **get** a job.

We can change the order of the two clauses if we want to.
*My brother **would help** me with my homework if he **had** more time.*

When the *If* clause comes first, there is a comma after it.

3   The word *would* is often spoken as *'d*. We can write it like this in informal writing, too. Also **would not** is often spoken as **wouldn't**.

4   When we use the verb *to be* in the *if* clause of second conditional sentences, we usually use *were* for all persons, including *I* and *he/she/it*. This is especially true in the phrase *If I were you* …
*If **I were** older, **I'd live** in my own apartment.*

Unit 15

Past perfect

1 We use the past perfect when we need to make it clear that one action happened **before** another action in the past.
*When I <u>arrived</u> at Jim's house, the party **had started**. (= The party started **before** I arrived.)*

Compare this with:
*When I <u>arrived</u> at Jim's house, the party **started**. (= I arrived, and **then** the party started.)*

2 We form the past perfect with *had/hadn't (had not)* + the past participle of the main verb.
*I didn't see Jane because she **had gone** out.*

3 When we use words like *before* and *after* in the past, it is often not necessary to use the past perfect because *before* and *after* make it clear which action happened first.
*The party <u>started</u> **before** I <u>arrived</u>.   We <u>got</u> to the train station **after** the train <u>left</u>.*

4 We often use the words *already* and *just* with the past perfect. They go between *had* and the main verb.
*I didn't go to the theater with them because I'<u>d</u> **already** <u>seen</u> the show.*

Unit 16

Reported statements

1 When we report what someone said in the past, we use reported speech. In reported speech, we use verbs like *say* or *tell*, and change some of the things that the person actually said.
*"I'<u>m</u> hungry," my sister said. → My sister **said (that) she was** hungry.*

2 We can use the word *that* between *said* or *told (me)* and the rest of the sentence, or we can leave it out.
*I said **that** I didn't want a hamburger. OR I said I didn't want a hamburger.*

3 We often change the verb tense between direct speech and reported speech, like this:

Direct speech		Reported speech
Simple present (continuous)	→	Simple past (continuous)
Simple past (continuous)	→	Past perfect (continuous)
Present perfect	→	Past perfect
am/is/are going to	→	*was/were going to*
can/can't	→	*could/couldn't*
will/won't	→	*would/wouldn't*

Third conditional

1 We use the third conditional to talk about unreal, imaginary situations in the past.
If you had told the teacher, she wouldn't have been angry. (= You <u>didn't tell</u> the teacher, and she <u>was</u> angry.)

2 Sentences in the third conditional also have two clauses: an *If* clause and a main clause.

If clause	Main clause
If + past perfect	*would have / wouldn't have* + main verb
*If my brother **had told** me,*	*I **would've known**.*
*If the team **hadn't played** so badly,*	*they **wouldn't have lost**.*

3 We can change the order of the two clauses if we want to.
*I **would have known** if my brother **had told** me.*
*The team **wouldn't have lost** if they **hadn't played** so badly.*

4 When the *If* clause is first, there's comma after it. There is no comma when the main clause is first.

Notes

Notes

Notes

Notes

Notes

Notes

Notes

Thanks and acknowledgments

The authors would like to thank a number of people whose support has proved invaluable during the planning, writing and production process of *American English in Mind*.

First of all we would like to thank the numerous teachers and students in many countries of the world who have used the first edition of *English in Mind*. Their enthusiasm for the course, and the detailed feedback and valuable suggestions we got from many of them were an important source of inspiration and guidance for us in developing the concept and in the creation of *American English in Mind*.

In particular, the authors and publishers would like to thank the following teachers who gave up their valuable time for classroom observations, interviews and focus groups:

Brazil
Warren Cragg (ASAP Idiomas); Angela Pinheiro da Cruz (Colégio São Bento; Carpe Diem); Ana Paula Vedovato Maestrello (Colégio Beatíssima Virgem Maria); Natália Mantovanelli Fontana (Lord's Idiomas); Renata Condi de Souza (Colégio Rio Branco, Higienópolis Branch); Alexandra Arruda Cardoso de Almeida (Colégio Guilherme Dumont Villares / Colégio Emilie de Villeneuve); Gisele Siqueira (Speak Up); Ana Karina Giusti Mantovani (Idéia Escolas de Línguas); Maria Virgínia G. B. de Lebron (UFTM / private lessons); Marina Piccinato (Speak Up); Patrícia Nero (Cultura Inglesa / Vila Mariana); Graziela Barroso (Associação Alumni); Francisco Carlos Peinado (Wording); Maria Lúcia Sciamarelli (Colégio Divina Providencia / Jundiaí); Deborah Hallal Jorge (Nice Time Language Center); Lilian Itzicovitch Leventhal (Colégio I. L. Peretz); Dulcinéia Ferreira (One Way Línguas); and Priscila Prieto and Carolina Cruz Marques (Seven Idiomas).

Colombia
Luz Amparo Chacón (Gimnasio Los Monjes); Mayra Barrera; Diana de la Pava (Colegio de la Presentación Las Ferias); Edgar Ardila (Col. Mayor José Celestino Mutis); Sandra Cavanzo B. (Liceo Campo David); Claudia Susana Contreras and Luz Marína Zuluaga (Colegio Anglo Americano); Celina Roldán and Angel Torres (Liceo Cervantes del Norte); Nelson Navarro; Maritza Ruiz Martín; Francisco Mejía, and Adriana Villalba (Colegio Calasanz).

Ecuador
Paul Viteri (Colegio Andino, Quito); William E. Yugsan (Golden Gate Academy – Quito); Irene Costales (Unidad Educativa Cardinal Spellman Femenino); Vinicio Sanchez and Sandra Milena Rodríguez (Colegio Santo Domingo de Guzmán); Sandra Rigazio and María Elena Moncayo (Unidad Educativa Tomás Moro, Quito); Jenny Alexandra Jara Recalde and Estanislao Javier Pauta (COTAC, Quito); Verónica Landázuri and Marisela Madrid (Unidad Educativa "San Francisco de Sales"); Oswaldo Gonzalez and Monica Tamayo (Angel Polibio Chaves School, Quito); Rosario Llerena and Tania Abad (Isaac Newton, Quito); María Fernanda Mármol Mazzini and Luis Armijos (Unidad Educativa Letort, Quito); and Diego Bastidas and Gonzalo Estrella (Colegio Gonzaga, Quito).

Mexico
Connie Alvarez (Colegio Makarenko); Julieta Zelinski (Colegio Williams); Patricia Avila (Liceo Ibero Mexicano); Patricia Cervantes de Brofft (Colegio Frances del Pedregal); Alicia Sotelo (Colegio Simon Bolivar); Patricia Lopez (Instituto Mexico, A.C.); Maria Eugenia Fernandez Castro (Instituto Oriente Arboledas); Lilian Ariadne Lozano Bustos (Universidad Tecmilenio); Maria del Consuelo Contreras Estrada (Liceo Albert Einstein);

Alfonso Rene Pelayo Garcia (Colegio Tomas Alva Edison); Ana Pilar Gonzalez (Instituto Felix de Jesus Rougier); and Blanca Kreutter (Instituto Simon Bolivar).

Our heartfelt thanks go to the *American English in Mind* team for their cooperative spirit, their many excellent suggestions and their dedication, which have been characteristic of the entire editorial process: Paul Phillips, Amy E. Hawley, Kelley Perrella, Eric Zuarino, Pam Harris, Kate Powers, Brigit Dermott, Kate Spencer, Heather McCarron, Keaton Babb, Roderick Gammon, Hugo Loyola, Howard Siegelman, Colleen Schumacher, Margaret Brooks, Kathryn O'Dell, Genevieve Kocienda, Lisa Hutchins, and Lynne Robertson.

We would also like to thank the teams of educational consultants, representatives and managers working for Cambridge University Press in various countries around the world. Space does not allow us to mention them all by name here, but we are extremely grateful for their support and their commitment.

In Student's Book 2, thanks go to David Crystal for the interview in Unit 9, and to Jon Turner for giving us the idea of using the story of Ulises de la Cruz in Unit 15.

Thanks to the team at Pentacor for giving the book its design; the staff at Full House Productions for the audio recordings; and Lightning Pictures and Mannic Media for the video.

Last but not least, we would like to thank our partners, Mares and Adriana, for their support.

The publishers are grateful to the following illustrators: Kel Dyson c/o Bright Agency, Dylan Gibson, Graham Kennedy, Laura Martinez c/o Sylvie Poggio, Mark Watkinson c/o Illustration

The publishers are grateful to the following for permission to reproduce photographic material:

Key: l = left, c = center, r = right, t = top, b = bottom

Alamy/Lynden Pioneer Museum p 17 (tr); Corbis/©David Ball/amanaimages p 29 (t), /©Bettmann p 75 (t), /©Bloomimage p 93 (bl), /©Andrew Brusso p 84, /©Jerry Cooke p 41 (br), /©Edith Held p 93 (cr), /©ROB & SAS p 93 (cl), /©Turba p 41; Education Photos/John Walmsley p 72 (A, D); FLPA/Minden Pictures/Mike Parryp 38; Getty Images/AFP/EVARISTO SA p 41 (l), /AFP/ Timothy Clary p 41 (tc), /Carlos Alvarez p 68, /Hulton Archive p 75 (b), /Photographer's Choice/Jeff Hunter p 28, /Photographer's Choice/Robert Manella p 72 (B), /Riser/Sara Wight p 72 (C), /Time & Life Pictures p 78, /WireImage/Vera Anderson p 70; iStockphoto/Yuri Arcurs p 42, The Kobal Collection/Film4/Celador Films/Pathe International p 96; Masterfile p 44; ©Robin Meldrum/ MSF, 2008, Democratic Republic of Congo p 77; PhotoLibrary.com/age fotostock/Juan Carlos Munoz p 51, /Stockbroker/Monkey Business Images Ltd p 22; Planetary Visions Ltd/Science Photo Library p 29 (b); Press Association Images/AP/Dolores Ochoa R. p 48Rex Features/David Fisher p 87; Shutterstock Images/Nejat p 17 (l), /Serbin Dmitry p 17 (br).
Getty Images/Carlsson, Peter/Johner Images p05; Getty Images/Comstock Images p6; Loc8tor Ltd. p12 (t); TrackItBack.com Inc. p12 (b); AP Photo/Sal Veder p54; Getty Images/Ben Fink Photo Inc.; Botanica p60; Getty Images/Marc Bryan-Brown/WireImage p64; Getty Images/J. Vespa/WireImage p92; Getty Images/Alan Danaher/The Image Bank p93 (tr)

The publishers are grateful to the following for their assistance with commissioned photographs: Mannic Media